The Mind of A Practitioner

Dharma Words (II)

Venerable Master Hsing Yun

Translated by
Venerable Miao Hsi and Cherry Lai

Buddha's Light Publishing
3456 S. Glenmark Drive
Hacienda Heights, CA 91745, U.S.A.
Tel: (626) 923-5144
Fax: (626) 923-5145
E-mail: info@blpusa.com
Website: www.blpusa.com

© 2007 Buddha's Light Publishing

Venerable Master Hsing Yun
Translated and edited by Venerable Miao Hsi and Cherry Lai
Edited by Edmond Chang and Robert Smitheram
Cover design by Dung Trieu
Sculpture "Contemplation" on the cover by Zhang Yuwei

ISBN-10: 1-932293-26-4
ISBN-13: 978-1-932293-26-5

    Library of Congress Cataloging-in-Publication Data

Xingyun, da shi.
 The mind of a practitioner / by Hsing Yun ; translated by Miao Hsi
and Cherry Lai.
    p. cm. -- (Dharma words : 2)
Translation of selections from Chinese.
ISBN 978-1-932293-26-5 (pbk. : alk. paper)
1. Fo Guang Shan Buddhist Order--Doctrines. 2. Religious life--
Buddhism. 3. Humanistic Buddhism. I. Hsi, Miao. II. Lai, Cherry.
III. Title. IV. Series.

BQ9800.F6392X554568 2007
294.3'444--dc22

                        2007000309

Acknowledgments

$\mathbf{W}$e received a lot of help from many people and we want to thank them for their efforts in making the publication of this book possible. We especially appreciate Venerable Tzu Jung, the Chief Executive of the Fo Guang Shan International Translation Center (F.G.S.I.T.C.), Venerable Hui Chi, Abbot of Hsi Lai Temple; Venerable Yi Chao for their guidance and support; Venerable Miao Hsi and Cherry Lai for their translation; Edmond Chang and Robert Smitheram for their editing; Kevin Hsyeh and Pey-Rong Lee for proofreading and preparing the manuscript for publication; and Dung Trieu for her book and cover design. Our appreciation also goes to everyone who has supported this project from its conception to its completion.

CONTENTS

Preface

I can think of no better summary and introduction to this book that what Master Hsing Yun says himself within its pages: "When we can experience the truth of the Dharma in everyday matters, it is true cultivation."

This book addresses the common problems and situations we all face in our hectic and complicated lives in this modern world, whether these are our personal relationships, family concerns, financial problems, health issues, and so on. The topics covered within these pages offer us specific attitudes and behaviors we can adopt that are not only beneficial for the matters at hand, but also further our spiritual cultivation as a whole. The outward manifestations of spiritual practice such as religious services and ceremonials, or specific methods of cultivation like chanting and meditation, can sometimes lead us to ignore how the common and everyday incidents in our lives can really call upon us to apply our spiritual principles in an effective manner. Like water that can slowly and imperceptibly wear away even the hardest rock, the course of our lives from birth, old age, sickness, and death is formed by how we choose to act and respond to these small, everyday matters in life. Something as minute and intangible as a single thought can have grave implications, and yet we hardly realize it, or perhaps even discount its effect. This is why the Buddhist teaching of karma is so important.

Karma means "action," but it is often confused with such notions as destiny or fate, which are actually quite different. karma is the law of cause and effect, the operation of causality as it relates to the formation of our lives as epitomized by the expression, "one reaps what one sows." Specifically in Buddhism, karma relates to the actions of one's body, speech, and mind; in that how we act, how we speak, and even how we think slowly and imperceptibly create the life we experience. A negative thought repeated billions of times, day after day, can create a rut so deep in one's life that it becomes an unconscious and habitual attitude, something that can color and distort one's life in unimaginable ways. Given innumerable lifetimes over countless eons of time, the accumulative effects of even these mental actions can be quite devastating. This is why Master Hsing Yun is constantly asking us to consider and examine our attitudes and behavior as we live our daily lives.

However, it must be underscored the karma does not mean "punishment." Indeed, nothing could be further from the truth. The Law of Karma is something we can consciously employ to change our lives at all levels of experience. Besides the more cautionary advice that Master Hsing Yun offers to avoid difficulty and suffering, he goes on to give guidance as to how we can bring positive qualities into our experience, as indicated by such topics as the "Four Joys in Life," "The Way to Success," the "Keys to a Long Life," and so on. Karma is the operation of cause and effect, and so a positive cause will bring about a positive effect. Joy and happiness do not simply fall from the sky for no reason, they come as the result of our behavior and action. Everything we experience in life comes to us through the power of karma, both the bad and the good, and we turn away from the bad and towards the good by the way we act, speak, and think. This is the hopeful message that

Master Hsing Yun is constantly asking us to consider very carefully.

Readers will also appreciate the practical and easily accessible style in which Master Hsing Yun offers his advice and guidance; lightly sprinkled with quotations from classical texts. One can meander at one's own pace, jumping forward or moving back, or pausing here and there along the way. But perhaps the most important thing to remember is give yourself time to ponder and reflect upon the topics addressed; the words may appear simple and straightforward, but their meaning is quite profound, so keep this book handy.

Robert H. Smitheram, Ph.D.
Translator and Editor
Buddha's Light Publishing

The Mind of A Practitioner

Dharma Words (II)

What the Wise Seek

Most people seek something from others all the time, from friends, their parents, the community, the country, various deities, and the Buddha. However, wise people will never seek as much from others as they would from themselves. If we cannot even seek improvement in ourselves, how can we possibly ask others for help? The following are some explanations on what the wise seek:

1. Seek to be proper in our conduct. *The Book of Rites* says, "Etiquette begins with correcting our actions, bringing our expression in order, and speaking the right words." We should do what is right when we act, speak, and think. We should not be rude or reckless. Our behavior should be poised, courteous, and unpretentious. In dealing with people and situations, we also need to conduct ourselves properly, neither being fawning nor arrogant. All in all, there are rules to follow in all our daily activities. As Mencius asserted, "Without the right ruler or compass, we can never make a proper square or circle." Similarly, with rules and regulations to guide us, we can enhance our character, poise, and image.

2. Seek right views in our belief. People cannot be without religion. No matter what faith or thinking we may follow, we should have right views as to our beliefs. Without right views, we will be easily swayed by whatever trend is in vogue. As we blindly follow along, we can become lost in life and become trapped by some superstition or cult. Therefore, without right views as the beacon in religious faith, we will be like a ship lost in the vast ocean, not knowing where we will end up. Therefore, we must have right views in our belief.

3. Seek to be diligent in our work. Benjamin Franklin said, "Leisure is time for doing something useful; this leisure the diligent man will obtain, but the lazy man never." No matter which profession we may pursue, it is of the utmost importance that we should strive to work hard. If there is gold flowing in the river, but we are reluctant to work hard, we will be too lazy to even pick it up. According to a saying, "Diligence is the path; complacency is the edge of the cliff; laziness is the grave." If we work hard in every matter, there is nothing we cannot complete, since diligence is the sole path to success.

4. Seek simplicity in our lifestyle. If we indulge ourselves in decadence and are complacent and wasteful in our everyday life, then no matter how much wealth we possess, the day will come when all is spent. Wang Yongqing may be the richest man in Taiwan, but he has been washing with the same towel for years. Therefore, truly successful people inevitably seek simplicity in life. Thus for them, clothes are only for keeping warm and food for satiating the pangs of hunger. Their home only needs to be reasonably comfortable. When we have cultivated the habit of simplicity in our lifestyle, we can rid ourselves of indulgence and wastefulness.

The *Book of Rites* asserts, "One cannot expand one's arrogance; one cannot indulge one's cravings." A wise person does not seek pleasure for the moment or look for temporary comfort. He or she does not jeopardize the loss of morals and right conduct over sensual pleasures. Through the ages, the wise have displayed their capacity through their purity of mind and simplicity in life. Therefore, we should always be mindful what the wise seek.

The Wise Do Not Contend

In life, it is very important to know others, but also oneself as well; not only theory, but also practice. Moreover, we must not only see things from one perspective, but also from its opposite. Only then will we not contend with people, not feel wronged, and be able to live in peace. The following suggestions are offered to help us emulate the wise and not contend with others:

1. Do not contend for wealth with people who enjoy hoarding money. There are many rich people in the world, and some may be as rich as a nation. But because they only know how to hoard and accumulate wealth, instead of appreciating how money is only truly owned when it is well spent. In this, they are actually poor. When they put money in the bank, they worry every day that their savings will be stolen. As a result, their lifetime of savings are never used by themselves for any good purpose. People like that are greedy, attached, and foolish. Though having money is good fortune, knowing how to spend it well is wisdom. Therefore, we should not just hoard money but should know how to use it well.

2. Do not contend for position with people who aggressively climb the social ladder. Some people anxiously scheme and plan for power and position, ever reaching for a higher status. However, we need not feel envious nor wronged, because achievements in life are not assessed by how high our position is. Instead, we need to have morals, make positive connections, and practice benevolence in order to gain the approval of others. Otherwise, in the ebb and flow of life, where would we

find the true meaning of life once power and status are lost?

3. Do not contend for fame with people who shrewdly conceal their shortcomings. Some people are good at covering up their faults and exaggerating their strengths, all for the sake of gaining fame and fortune. Xunzi said, "A righteous person does not cover up his strengths and weaknesses but stands on his true worth." When we can show our true self, we have integrity. In Chinese history, those who claimed undue credit or contended for an undeserved position often ended up killed by the ruler, while those who retreated after accomplishments lived out their years in peace. Therefore, as long as we stand on the substance of our virtue, there is really no need to contend for credit and fame.

4. Do not contend for respect with people who are arrogant. Some people think very highly of themselves, and they demand others to pay them every respect. We need not be upset with people like those or ask them to reciprocate by treating others well. As Mencius said, "People always love those who love others; people respect those who respect others." As long as we have a noble character and treat others with respect, we will naturally gain their respect. If we keep insisting that other people show us respect, we will often receive the opposite in return. Therefore, we need not contend with arrogant people for respect.

If we are not really learned or skilled but only seek an empty name, position or power, we will one day fall from any height we may have attained. Therefore, the wise only strive to improve their ethics and character instead of superficial glory.

Getting Along with People

How to get along with people is an art in itself. We cannot just follow our own likes and dislikes in dealing with others. We should show a keen appreciation for the natural sentiments of people. Every person wants to be respected, understood, praised, and accepted. As *Humble Table, Wise Fare* says, "Those who greet others with a kind face will gain harmony. Those who get along with others with a humble attitude will gain esteem. Those who treat others with a respectful mind will gain deference. Those who praise others with words will gain human affinity." Accordingly, what follows are four ways to get along well with people:

1. Counter obstinacy with gentleness. People possess a range of personalities. Some are humble and gentle, while others may be arrogant and abrasive. Chan Master Keqin of the Song Dynasty once said, "People for the most part are inherently benevolent, so they should treat each other with compassion and gentleness. In treating others with a benevolent nature, we can inhabit equanimity and peace." In fact, gentleness is the best prescription in dealing with all matters, for it can put out the fire of anger. Some people may be strong-willed, but if we are equally stubborn with them, we would only end up creating a no-win situation. The best way to counter force is to apply gentleness. In other words, if you are rude to me, I should instead be polite and show respect to you; if you are arrogant towards me, I should respond with humility. As the saying goes, "Teeth break easily because they are hard, so we should treasure gentleness." When we engage others with gentleness, we will face no obstacles in getting along them.

2. Counter meanness with tolerance. *Humble Table, Wise Fare* states, "With a broad mind, every road is open; With a mean heart, thorny bushes pervade." Some people can be mean and calculating. They are hard on others and are never willing to compromise their self-interest. When we encounter any family member, friend or coworker who behaves in this manner, the best strategy is to treat that person with magnanimity and tolerance. Such an approach can resolve all disputes and alleviate all grudges, leading us to more harmonious relationships. There is a saying, "We should be single-minded in work, yet broad-minded in being human." When we can unlock the narrow heart with the key of tolerance, and rest our body and mind on the bed of forgiveness, our world will be much broader.

3. Counter coldness with passion. In an age that emphasizes color and sound, people often express themselves vividly, loudly, and vibrantly. To emulate the glowing warmth of the sun, we should always smile and speak in kind words when dealing with others. Especially when we are dealing with those who are cold and unfeeling, we should be as passionate as the sun in using our warmth to melt their iciness. "A focused mind can cultivate potential; a passionate heart can melt coldness." A person who can generate warmth within a group is most wise.

4. Counter anger with compassion. Buddhist sutras state, "Anger is the fire in the mind that can burn away a forest of merits." When anger arises, it can block a person's good sense, like dark clouds covering the moon. It is indeed like a wild fire that can destroy a whole forest. Anger can spoil our good deeds, ruin our love, provoke a disaster, and squander our merits. Therefore, practition-

ers of the Way should first learn to guard against anger. We must first eradicate anger before we can even speak of the Way. If we are easily irritated and upset, we will just as easily make more enemies. In dealing with people filled with anger, we can only use compassion and patience to calm them down. Compassion and loving kindness are indomitable shields. In life, we should not only resolve disputes with reasoning, but also dissolve conflict with compassion.

All in all, in getting along with others, we should be gentle, tolerant, loving, and compassionate.

Dealing with Difficult People

In practicing Buddhism, we first need to learn how to live in the world. But before we can truly know how to face the world, we need to learn how to handle difficult people and situations. The ancients were patient and diligent in teaching their students. They used all kinds of skillful means with no intention of giving up on anyone. Throughout history, bodhisattvas have responded to requests for help from everywhere, acting as a ferry to transport people across the ocean of suffering; nor do they give up on any sentient being either. We should learn from the resolve of the wise and virtuous by being able to undertake what is difficult and tolerate what is hard to bear. We need to accomplish what we perceive as difficult and get along with people we perceive as troublesome. The following are some guidelines on how to handle difficult people:

1. Inspire deceitful people with sincerity. In today's society, there are many people who cheat and deceive. They are crafty and fraudulent, making use of people's greed or sympathy to make a profit. There are also cult leaders who employ mystic powers or ideas as a way of cheating people out of their savings. Many marketers offer misleading advertisements or dazzling gimmicks as a way to sell their products. If we come across people like these, we naturally should not allow them to deceive us. Instead, we must educate and inspire them with our sincerity and honesty.

2. Influence bad-tempered people with gentleness. When faced with people who are violent and bad-tempered, we cannot be like them by trying to overcome violence with violence. This will only tend to make matter much

worse. Therefore, when they get angry, we must be even calmer and gentler in order to influence them with equanimity. We have to help them subdue their angry and violent tendencies.

3. Urge deviant people to improve with loyalty and righteousness. There are inevitably unwholesome people full of deviant views, who show no integrity towards others or loyalty towards country. When they speak to others, all they express are immoral and devious views. We must urge them to change their ways with our own integrity and impress them with our righteousness. They may eventually appreciate our right views and thinking as well as our sense of loyalty and ethics. Thus, they may end up sharing our way and follow the right path.

4. Guide stubborn people with tolerance. Some people have deeply rooted bad habits and refuse any guidance from others. We cannot ignore or give up on them. There was once an incorrigible fellow living in a Chan monastery. The rest of the practitioners wanted to evict him, but the monk in charge said, "If we throw him out of the monastery, people in society will be hurt. When even a monastery cannot get him to improve, where can he go to change his ways?" Therefore, when faced with corrupt people, we should tolerate them and guide them with compassion. When shame arises in them, they will change for the better.

In dealing with people, we cannot just choose those who are good, kind, and righteous, and we should not reject those who have bad habits and unwholesome behavior. Instead, we have to treat others the way we want to be treated, and place the same demands on ourselves as we do on others. With this kind of tolerance, we will not find anyone too difficult to handle nor any matter too hard to accomplish.

Four Kinds of People

Having an education helps us to be understanding and reasonable, so that we know how to conduct ourselves. However, if we lack common sense or the ability to see clearly the ways of the world, then we have not thoroughly learned how to be truly human. This is difficult because there are so many kinds of people. While some people dedicate themselves to promoting the public good, others are selfish. While some act courageously to lend a helping hand, others cowardly ignore the general welfare. Just as there are cunning and deceitful or frivolous and shallow people, there are also righteous and steady ones. After all, "The same rice can nurture a hundred different types of people" as a Chinese saying goes. Let's examine the following four basic kinds:

1. Indifferent Outsiders: This represents the kind of people who face any matter or situation with indifference. In their minds, "there is always someone taller to keep the sky from falling." Because of their attitude as outsiders, they have no interest or concern for world events and social problems. In their indifference however, they neglect the fact that everything is a product of causes and conditions. There is a relationship of interdependence in the world where everyone and everything is interconnected. "If the nest is overturned, there won't be any whole eggs left." Therefore, when the country is in trouble or society becomes riddled with problems, it is imperative for us to be an engaged insider rather than an indifferent outsider.

2. Heartless Spectators: It is common for some people to take a wait-and-see attitude when others are in trouble. They will simply stand by and do nothing. For example,

they will never risk their lives in a neighborhood fire or sympathize with the sufferings of others; and when a stranger falls on the pavement, they will not offer any help. Even if all it takes is to extend a helping hand, they will remain indifferent and still walk away, for they are callous in their role as spectators. Thus, if we lose our mind of loving-kindness and compassion, having no care or sympathy for anyone, we become cold-blooded and rob ourselves of our humanity, reducing ourselves to the state of mere animals. Hence, if we value ourselves as worthy human beings, we must have a caring heart and not be a heartless spectator.

3. Unscrupulous Opportunists: These are people who are good at pleasing both parties and jumping on the bandwagon. On the surface, they seem to have gained advantages from both sides and will achieve success one way or another. In reality, they have gained nothing by straddling both sides of the fence and being unscrupulous when it comes to right and wrong. Because they lack credibility in their words and deeds, people will find them unreliable and untrustworthy. Therefore, if we want to be trustworthy and taken seriously, we must be scrupulous in our actions and our principles.

4. Humble Achievers: The best kind of people are those who have achieved success but do not take any credit. They never hesitate to contribute wholeheartedly and do everything within their power to facilitate another's success. Once the goal is accomplished, they will make a quick exit from the limelight and will transfer merit and prestige to others without any sense of attachment. Because of people like that, society is able to grow and progress.

In contrast, some people will refuse to step down, fearing that others may want to share in their gains. Due to their unwillingness to resign their power and position at the appropriate time, they only end up being the object of others' contempt. Ultimately, such people fail. Therefore, a wise person will always recognize the most opportune time to step away.

To learn is to conduct ourselves properly and to be considerate of others by putting ourselves in their shoes. If we can walk in another's shoes, we will have no trouble progressing in our resolve to give all we have for the sake of others. Only when we are willing to help others in their achievements will success be within our reach. What kind of person should we strive to be? The above are four categories from which to choose.

Four Grades of People

Nowadays, people are interested in their emotional quotient or EQ, but most still have a lot of trouble keeping their emotions in check. Although some people are very capable in their abilities, their EQ leaves much to be desired. Moreover, there are those who are both incapable and temperamental, and naturally, will not be accepted by others. While some people are praised for their outstanding abilities and gentle disposition, other less capable but mild-tempered ones are tolerated because they can work easily with others and are eager to learn.

A person's greatness cannot be measured by ability alone, for we must consider his or her capacity for tolerance. All people are capable in one area or another, and can learn various skills or knowledge, but not everyone is capable of cultivating tolerance. A capacity for tolerance is hard to foster, for one cannot harbor any jealousy or bad temper. Based on such a capability and capacity for tolerance, we can distinguish the following grades of people:

1. People of the first grade possess great ability and an even temper. A teacher who is a good educator will never lose patience in searching for the best teaching method. On the other hand, a teacher who often loses his or her temper and resorts to punishment to control the students lacks sufficient teaching skills. Therefore, in order for us to be the best we can be, we must develop our potential and foster our abilities. More importantly, we need to discipline ourselves in controlling our emotions and remaining calm.

2. People of the second grade possess great ability and a quick temper. People who are perfectionists tend to have a volatile temper, because they are impatient with those

they consider less capable and incompatible. In working with others, they get easily irritated when others cannot match their skills. They resort to unleashing their temper to correct others, and nagging them to meet their standards. Although it is undesirable for us to lose our temper, it is tolerable sometimes if our intentions are good. However, if our anger is unwarranted, it only creates animosity. Hence, a person of great ability but with a quick temper can only be considered second grade.

3. People of the third grade possess little ability and no temper. They are ordinary people who are self-conscious of their shortcomings and inabilities. Because of their awareness, they are usually calm and indifferent to situations that are provocative or confrontational. Since they deem themselves not as capable or talented as others, they will not lose their temper easily and do their best to appease others.

4. People of the fourth grade possess no ability and a bad temper. Although they have no ability and never accomplish anything in life, they are still extremely harsh and demanding of others. Because of their low EQ, they are not well-liked by others regardless of their position in life.

Truly capable people do not need to be temperamental in the way they lead or teach. If we are wise and virtuous, we must lead by example, influence others with ethics, and tolerate those around us with magnanimity. Therefore, in assessing ourselves, to which of the above grades do we belong?

The Art of Reading People

"One's appearance is the product of one's mind; one's countenance is the result of one's mental state." Although physiognomy is the art of judging one's fate and future from facial features, true destiny is determined by one's inner qualities and outward conduct. Therefore, if we want to master the art of reading people, we must first learn how to judge another's sincerity, generosity, abilities, and courage. Some guidelines are listed below:

1. Judge character by how people respond to enticement. "A virtuous person will never seek profit illicitly while an immoral person will abandon every principle for personal gain." Hence, we can judge a person's character by enticing him or her with great wealth and observe their response. If a person is virtuous and follows the right path, he or she will exhibit an inherent sense of righteousness by refusing to accept any unwarranted benefits. On the other hand, an unscrupulous person will scramble like flies after honey for the smallest profit regardless of the consequences. Therefore, in the face of gain and benefit, it is impossible for people to hide one's true nature of virtue or selfishness.

2. Measure morality by how people handle matters. People who are kind and honest will never expose others' shortcomings for their own advantage. They are willing to take a loss and not insist on receiving what is due. However, people short on character will disregard the reputation of others for the sake of personal gain. Therefore, one way for us to gauge the degree of one's moral character is to work with that person and observe how he or she handles matters.

3. Determine ability by how people set plans. An intelligent person will undoubtedly know the importance of planning as well as having an entire arsenal of tactics at their disposal. In addition to offering honest opinions, he or she is very adept at using strategies. On the other hand, a person of average intelligence and ability lacks the required patience and does not excel in reasoning. Therefore, in order for us to correctly determine a person's abilities and wisdom, we must first know how adept he or she is at planning.

4. Recognize courage by how people use force. While a troublemaker is a person who lacks insight, a courageous person has the ability to bear great responsibility. One way for us to test courage is to see how people react under pressure. If a person is a coward, he or she will be afraid to express their opinion. However, showing no fear means that one is a person of great courage.

Throughout history, there have been many extraordinary horses that were overlooked by ordinary trainers. Only when they were trained by the finest of trainers would their true abilities can be made apparent. Similarly, there are many smart and talented people in this world, but there are not too many people who are well-versed in the art of reading the qualities of others and putting them to good use. Therefore, it is imperative for managers and employers to be astute in their judgment of their staff and employees so that they can assign the right task to the right person.

The Source of Human Power

What society needs most nowadays is to increase energy resources, but where can we find them? The sources of energy can be found in the natural world – in the wind, the ocean, and the sun. While solar panels, wind-driven generators, and hydraulic power plants are resources for electrical power, it is in fact the human "mind" that represents the most powerful resource. As the mind can summon forth unimaginable power, what are the mental resources upon which we can rely for strength and power? The following are some definitions:

1. Pressure is the power for motivation. Pressure is unavoidable in our daily life, and we need not react negatively to it. We should instead see it in a positive light as the impetus for developing our potential. For example, during the Period of the Warring States in China around the fourth century BCE, the weak kingdoms needed to overcome the mounting pressure imposed by the larger states through reform and change. Therefore, pressure can be the motivation that propels us forward toward success.

2. Resistance is the power for progress. When we park a vehicle on a steep slope, we might need to place a chock behind the rear wheels to prevent the vehicle from rolling down. When resistance is properly applied, it can be a force that prevents regression and promotes advancement. It is like the art of gardening: flowers bloom more beautifully after a good pruning. Thus, resistance can be a strong motivation for development and growth.

3. Listening is the power of empathy for others. It is very important for us to listen well in getting along with people. If we are good listeners, we will be aware of the significance of what is said and the intention of the speaker. Moreover, we will be able to receive what we hear more positively. In turn, this will allow us to foster a greater appreciation for the truth as well as for other people's opinions.

4. Wholeheartedness is the power for having no regrets. Success and failure are irrelevant as long as we have done our best in giving everything we have. "The virtue of a fine horse is to exert strength in accordance to its burden" teaches the *Discourses of the Buddha*. The same can be said of humans. If they work wholeheartedly to improve themselves and to make progress, they will gain the power for having no regrets.

5. Perseverance is the power for judgment. Perseverance helps us to be consistent and steadfast in facing obstacles or setbacks. It allows us to endure by not giving up regardless of how difficult the situation may be. Thus, happiness will follow suffering as we reap the fruits of our labor. If we persevere in dealing with hardship, over time we will gain the power to judge more wisely.

6. Potential is the power for development. We all have potential, a bottomless treasure trove which is our inherent ability for growth and development. According to some accounts, even geniuses like Albert Einstein only tapped into five-percent of their brain's potential. Therefore, if we can realize every ounce of our potential, only the sky would be our limit.

7. Old age is the power for experience. It is a mistake to assume that old age is a sign of uselessness, and a harbinger of having one foot in the grave. In fact, a person of advanced age can be a wise individual – someone who has lived through time and accumulated experience along the way. Old age thus is the power of experience that none can deny.

8. Effort is the power for success. "Diligence leads to skillfulness and frolicking brings negligence to one's work; thoughtfulness gains success and carelessness brings failure in one's endeavors," said Han Yue, a literary giant of the Tang Dynasty. It explains the underlying truth of reaping what one has sown. As long as we are diligent with our efforts to till and weed, we will have better crops and bigger harvests. "Genius is one percent inspiration and 99 percent perspiration," remarked Thomas Edison. Therefore, effort grants us the power to succeed.

The source of human power is limitless and infinite. Sometimes it can be developed within solely by virtue of our strength, while at other times it depends upon external help. In general, there are eight sources of human power as indicated above.

Modern People

In the past, because traditional cultures tended to close themselves off from the outside and authoritarian governments were the norm, people lived in poverty and suffering. In the pursuit of liberty, democracy, wealth, and prosperity, people nowadays want to become modernized. Modernization signifies development, progress, renewal, adaptation, and upward mobility. Countries, societies, religions or individuals all need to keep pace with the changes in time and space by seeking progress on the path of modernization.

So what is modernization? Having an open attitude and the mentality to keep on learning is being modern. It is a willingness to rid ourselves of set views and to accept new ideas and realities. A mind that is active in making progress can help us improve constantly. Only in this way can we become a modern people who feels heart home in our own element. The following are some keys on how to become modern :

1. Read all manner of books. This is the first step. We should try to read the history of all ages, as well as astronomy, geography, art, literature, etc., because we need a broad knowledge in every field. In this multi-faceted, modern world, it is not enough to know about just one matter. In order to establish ourselves in the world, we have to cover all the bases before we can go on to specialize in one field. Reading as much as we can enables us to "See the ancient and modern times at a glance and touch the four seas in a moment." Reading widely is the prerequisite for becoming modern.

2. Travel the paths of the world. The ancients said, "Read ten-thousand volumes; travel ten-thousand miles. It glo-

rifies both self and other, and is of benefit to oneself."
Modern people should do the same. Besides reading, we
should actually appreciate different cultures and social
customs in order to gain personal experience and understand the reality of every country. We should be aware
of the thinking, spirit, and substance of the people of each
country and ethnicity. When we can travel to every corner of the world and tread on every land, for the whole
world is within our reach. Hence, modern people should
try to travel everywhere in the world.

3. Observe all the people in the world. There are all kinds
   of people in the world, and they have different skin color
   and life in various parts of the globe. They may be
   wealthy, poor, or appealing to our eyes. Their ways of
   speaking, their customs, faith and lifestyle can all vary
   dramatically depending upon on their nationality, ethnicity, family background, profession, and appearance.
   Modern people, therefore, should observe all people
   without bias, before they can truly understand the world.

4. Experience all matters in the world. The range of things
   that we can do in life is endless. Regardless of whether
   something is common, wonderful, new or difficult, it is
   to our benefit that we experience each one of them ourselves. "Without experiencing a matter, one fails to gain
   wisdom." Experience provides the most wisdom. Hence,
   living in today's world as modern people, we must be
   brave in taking up new challenges and experience all
   there is for us to learn.

In this progressive age, technology, knowledge, lifestyle
and thinking are all modernized. How do people keep up with the
pace in these modern times without being left out? How do we

become modern people? Clinging to the status quo is falling behind the times; we will be left behind if we do not progress fast enough. Therefore, to become truly modern, we need to follow the above four suggestions.

Ills of Modern People

Throughout history, different social problems have arisen at different stages of civilization. While the ancients were often burdened with the weight of tradition, modern people nowadays have to deal with the social ills of our times. While we may be making advancements in science and technology, our morality and our mind may have degenerated over time. People today often lack moral courage and fall short in righteousness and humility. Often what is left is apathy and suspicion among people, who rather than progress with the advancement of civilization, resort to exaggerated and unrealistic ambition, coupled with an unwillingness to assume honest hard work. The following are some of the common ills of modern people:

1. The ill of rashness and impulsiveness: The most serious ill of modern people is that they do not think carefully and lack common sense, causing them to rush into matters impulsively. With no consideration for anything or anyone, they do what they please and end up offending or violating many people as a consequence. Because in their self-righteousness they fail to recognize the importance of past causes and conditions and think little of how others feel, they often live with their own regrets when things do not go well. However, they tend to behave the same way the next time by acting as rashly and impulsively as before.

2. The ill of apathy: Modern people lack the warmth of those from the agricultural age. They do not offer encouragement or congratulations for the accomplishments of others and choose to look on coldly when others ask for help. For example, nowadays whenever there

is a car accident, people tend to watch from the sidelines, treating it as a spectacle, but not helping for fear of taking on any extra burden. It is as the Chinese saying goes, "Just sweeping the snow in front of one's door, with no regard for the frost on someone else's roof." Such people find it hard to offer others a simple word of comfort or encouragement when needed. We often hear people bemoan how the world has advanced in technology and made economic gains, but human sentiments have sadly turned cold and society apathetic.

3. The ill of indifference: Modern people may live right next door or across the street from one another for several decades without even knowing their neighbors, not to mention socializing with or showing care and concern for each other. The common ill of people these days is living within their own isolated world as if nothing else in the world has any connection or relation to them. Such people are loners fighting their own battles. While there is an abundance of material resources and opportunities, too many people today live as a lonely entity. Because of their indifference to human relationships, some people have become so frustrated and depressed that their existence is even worse than those living in a prison.

4. The ill of being heartless and unscrupulous: Another serious ill afflicting people today is being cold-hearted and ruthless. In pursuing personal gain, people fight over status and money with no regard to human sentiments or ethics. Because of their selfishness and ego, they place profit above morals and their personal needs over human relationships. In protecting their own benefits, they are capable of committing all sorts of unethical

acts. If this ill is not cured, it will be difficult to improve the norms of society.

We should not fear problems, but only fear not knowing what the problems are. When we discover the causes of our problems, we can prescribe the right treatment. We should never hide from problems or allow negative attitudes to persist. Hence, we need to pay more attention to the above-mentioned ills.

Interpersonal Relationships

Since humans are essentially social beings and are incapable of living apart from their fellow human beings, the subject of interpersonal relationships is an important field of study. In getting along with other people, we must first recognize the value or importance of human relationships. Moreover, in developing meaningful friendships, we must learn to appreciate the virtues of others while tolerating their weaknesses. We should not flaunt our own strength at the expense of others' weakness. Instead, it is imperative for us to respect others and help them in their achievements. There are four points to consider for a successful relationship:

1. Earn the respect of the virtuous with morals. We should never try to bribe or please those who are capable and wise with fame, fortune, or power. Instead, we should use our moral character and conduct to get along with them. Xunzi advocated, "The benevolent are easy to befriend but hard to take liberties with." Although the capable and the virtuous are easy to befriend, it is difficult for them to respect us if we have nothing to offer except frivolous and meaningless flattery. Therefore, it is important for us to earn the respect and admiration of those who are able and worthy by means of our moral character.

2. Win over the stubborn and the unwilling with skillful means. How should we get along with those who are naturally unruly, defiant, or insolent? It is through skillful means. To train a difficult horse, a trainer must first know its temperament well before they can proceed further. Sometimes, a free rein is necessary, while at other

times it is important to pull in the reins to guide the horse. Similarly, we cannot be rigid in our ways by constantly blaming and yelling at people who refuse to correct their mistakes. Instead, we should first try to win their respect and listen to their sentiments before giving proper advice. If we want to convince them, we must first deal with their problems and fulfill their needs. Hence, the best way for us to win over those who are stubborn in doing the wrong thing is to win them over tactfully with skillful means.

3. Encourage the seemingly simple and naive with diligence. When we are faced with people who are slower, simpler or more naive than us, how should we react? "We should value one's strength and tolerate one's weakness," said *The History of the Three Kingdoms* in explaining the importance of taking into account a person's abilities when making the best use of human resources. In other words, we must tolerate shortcomings of others in addition to taking full advantage of their strong points. For the less capable, we should assign tasks that are easier to accomplish, while also imparting methods to accomplish such tasks, so that they will have the confidence to tackle them on their own later on. Only with diligence can we encourage a strong sense of independence in those who are perceived to be simple and naive.

4. Teach obstinate and difficult people through strategy. Since we cannot simply ignore or avoid people who are stubborn, defiant or mean, we must find a way for them to accept us. For example, we can love and care for them in order to soften their stance and lessen their hostility. We can also encourage and praise them, so they can develop a sense of self-confidence. When appropriate,

we can even compel them to follow and listen to us by the power of authority. Hence, it is imperative for us to employ the right strategy in dealing with those who are stubborn and unruly.

Successful interpersonal relationships require us to better observe, follow, and treasure the causes and conditions that are present. In order to avoid conflict, we especially need to give each other more space. If we can eliminate confrontations and reduce frictions in our relationships, we can easily maintain a more open communication and complement one another well in what we do. Therefore, we should be aware of the guidelines above.

The Nexus of Interpersonal Relations

Humans are the most troublesome beings in this world. They are the subjects of a complicated nexus of relationships that combines various instances of "I," "you," and "he/she." Within this nexus of interpersonal relationships, each subject represents a unique character with their own personality, thought process, and point of view. Consequently, interactions within this nexus can produce many conflicts and disputes, so how are we supposed to gain peace and harmony? The following are four suggestions on how to improve the nexus of human relationships:

1. Replace self-serving with serving. Some Buddhists in the past, such as some arhats and Theravadans, were derided as being self-serving practitioners, for they only cared about their own deliverance from the endless cycles of rebirth and not about the suffering of others. It is indeed not the right way to practice. Master Cihang once said, "Do not seek personal liberation while even one person remains to be liberated." Therefore, we must view all beings as sharing the same destiny and mutual concern, and be willing to serve others. "It is impossible for one to be reborn in the Western Pure Land with insufficient meritorious virtues," teaches the *Amitabha Sutra*. Serving the public is to broadly sow the causes and conditions of good actions and merits. Hence, it is imperative for us to replace our focus on being self-serving with that of serving others.

2. Replace mysticism with diligent practice. In the past, it was common for some monastics to portray the teachings of the Buddha in a mystical and esoteric light. Accordingly, the Buddhist doctrines became very diffi-

cult to understand and almost impossible to propagate. In order for us to remedy this problem, we must replace mysticism with diligent practice; that is, we must personally put into practice the words of the Buddha. For example, "generosity," "loving-kindness," and "compassion" begin with oneself, since it is unfair to ask another person to achieve what we have failed to do ourselves. If we want to successfully convince others to follow and place their trust in us, we must set a good example with our own conduct. Hence, we need to replace mysticism with diligent practice.

3. Replace impersonal communication with personal contact. In today's world, personal exchange remains a necessity despite advancements in modern technology, which facilitate communication around the world. While humans depend on personal contact for social survival, countries must also rely on meaningful exchanges and diplomatic relations for peaceful coexistence. Personal contact fosters trust and lessens suspicion.

4. Replace empty words with concrete action. As the saying goes, "It is better to translate one principle into action than talk about many at length." It is important for us to put what we say in action. As Mencius taught, "Whatever we seek, we will obtain because we are the seeker." If we want to be successful, we must put forth the effort; likewise, if we are persistent and determined in our actions, we must avoid empty talk. Empty words are nothing but figments of our imagination. They are like trying to satisfy hunger by drawing a picture of a loaf of bread. This is why we should replace empty words with actual practice.

Although the problems within the nexus of human relationships are complicated, they are not unsolvable. We can best cope with them by heeding the above advice.

Four Don'ts in Relationships

People usually find it impossible to detach themselves from the love of family, friends, and lovers. Some people can deal with love easily and happily while others are trapped by it. The latter often exhaust themselves not knowing which direction their heads are turning and may even get into serious trouble because of it. A Qing scholar once warned that in making friends it is important to be "sincere, righteous, willing to accept disadvantages, and tolerant without being selfish or suspicious of others." Indeed, we need to exhibit magnanimity and mutual respect in every kind of love in order to get along well with different people, which is how we can avoid becoming mired in gains and losses or trapped over questions of right and wrong. The following are four things we must try and avoid in relationships:

1. Don't make enemies of unwholesome people. According to the saying, "The same kind of rice can nurture a hundred kinds of people." People are variably good, bad, kind, malicious, exemplary, common, wise, and foolish. Those who are good, kind or wise will not quibble over small matters with others. They do not even mind if they are neglected by others. However, if someone takes small advantages of unwholesome people or commits a transgression against them, they will bear a grudge. They will scheme to take revenge in order to get even. Accordingly, Guanzi, a famed scholar, explained, "One would rather offend the wise than provoke the crooked. In offending the wise, the grudge is light; in transgressing against the crooked, the trouble is deep." Therefore, not making enemies of unwholesome people is for our own protection, for they can be as dangerous as an explosive mine planted by our side.

2. Don't take advantage of friends. We should not just think of profiting from our friends. Friendship should be based on mutual trust, morality, righteousness, and an exchange of knowledge. It is not about calculating benefit, competing in fame and name, or battling abilities and wits. A Sui Dynasty philosopher once said, "Friendships based on power will end when power fails; friendships based on profit will fall apart when profits cease." Friendships need to be sustained by mutual respect and encouragement. We can never assume we have the right to take advantage of others wherever we go. Moreover, we should not look down on others or step on them. True friendship should be based on equality and on sharing glory and respect with one another.

3. Don't distance oneself from family and relatives. We cannot ignore our family and loved ones no matter how busy we are. We still need to find time to show our concern. Even if we have to go far away or immigrate to another country, we have to call or write, inquiring about their well being and sharing with them the small things in life. Everybody – children, teenagers, adults, and seniors – needs love and assistance from their family to support their growth and tend to their care. We must show gratitude and care for our family by keeping in touch. We should express genuine respect from our hearts and not simply dwell on superficial socializing.

4. Don't be overly attached to love. Regardless of what or who it is, investing too much of our emotions and feelings in an object of love is a form of constraint. Some people are infatuated with material objects and become bound by them. They may love plants and pets so much that when their beloved animal or tree dies, they grieve as

they would for their parents' death. Moreover, some people love their parents and family members so much that they become entangled in endless attachments because of it. Lovers suffer because they have become so consumed with love for their partners, that they may end up harming both self and others.

The Buddha spoke about "the suffering of encountering our enemies and the suffering of leaving our loved ones." The heart-wrenching pain of love comes from our possessiveness and strong attachment. Therefore, we need to play down both love and hate, and purify our love and attachments. When we can elevate our intense love for people and objects into making contributions and offering our service to others, we will be able to rid ourselves of such suffering.

"One will not have been born in the *Saha* world without strong love." People are beings of love and emotions. Our lives are attached to the love of family, friends, and lovers. How to interact positively and handle human relationships well within the different kinds of love certainly constitute the major lessons in life.

To Be Welcomed by Others

There is a phenomenon that often occurs at social functions, for when a certain person enters, the whole place is filled with laughter and friendliness. He or she can warm up a place and is welcomed by everyone anywhere he or she goes. On the other hand, there are others who can turn a warm and amiable atmosphere into something frigid as soon as they arrive, and such people are not welcomed anywhere. How do we become someone welcomed by others? The following are some considerations:

1. It is better to be liked than feared. Some supervisors or elders try to use their authority and status to gain respect through intimidating others. However, it is not always good to be authoritative and provoke fear in others. Since most people are afraid of offending powerful people, the latter usually become isolated in the end. It is better for us to be liked, for then people will want to get close to us and be our friend. At the very least, to be liked means that others consider us to be a good person.

2. It is better to be praised than merely liked. Sometimes, we may like a certain person, but we cannot tell exactly what we like about him or her. It is not sufficient to be liked by others merely by virtue of our common views and interests, our good looks, our temperament, or our acquiescence. To win others' praise, however, we must have strengths that others admire. If we like someone, we should be able to praise him or her for being compassionate, responsible, courteous, easy-going, fair, patient, and magnanimous at heart. People who are praised by others are often endowed with these good qualities.

3. It is better to be respected than merely praised. Being praised may mean we are capable and learned, but not necessarily respected by others. Respect is harder to come by, because it is based on our morals, poise, and conduct that others admire. It is better to be respected than praised, because when we earn people's respect, we will not only be liked, but will also be taken seriously.

4. It is better to be remembered than merely respected. We may respect someone, but once he or she leaves, we will forget about them over time. Being respected sometimes depends on the causes and conditions of staying in touch with others. People may respect us when they are together with us in the same place, but they may not think about us once we have left. However, being remembered can last a lifetime. Many friends may live in different places for decades, but they remember each other fondly just the same. Many noble examples and feats from the past are still etched deeply in the pages of history and survive into posterity as part of our collective memory. Therefore, being remembered is better than being respected.

Regardless of the level of our job or what ethnic group to which we belong, we all seek to be respected, be taken seriously, and looked upon as a popular person. However, it is easy to be welcomed and liked by others, but difficult to be respected. People may be feared, liked, accepted, or remembered. What is best? We can consider the above guidelines in deciding how to make ourselves welcomed by others.

People and Issues

Wherever there are people in the world, issues will arise. Whenever we consider people and issues, we realize they are indeed difficult and complicated to reconcile. However, we have to face and deal with many people and issues everyday. How should we handle them? The following are some guidelines:

1. We should maintain equanimity in dealing with conflict. Many conflicts result from people thinking they have a just cause. Everyone has their own point of view and ways of thinking, and they may even refuse to listen to others. How should we handle such situations? We must be just and treat them with equanimity. Zeng Guofan, a Qing Dynasty scholar, once said, "If our mind is not calm, we cannot be meticulous in self-reflection nor open to reason." Therefore, it is best to be calm and even-minded. There is no need to rush or be attached to any views, since reason will always prevail in the end.

2. We should show magnanimity in dealing with difficult people. We need to be bighearted because magnanimity generates good fortune. People who are tolerant and forgiving can turn a hostile situation into a peaceful one, thus gaining peace of mind and harmony. We must be especially bighearted when we are dealing with difficult people, for they may want to get even when offended, and may even take revenge on us through the use of power and chicanery. Therefore, in dealing with difficult people, we must be tolerant.

3. We should slow down in dealing with complex issues.

Issues can be big or small, urgent or less pressing, public or personal. While we have to deal with all of them, we do need to prioritize. There is an old saying, "Slow in dealing with major matters, and quick with small ones." Major issues mean those that are critical, carry a strong impact, and are difficult to handle. Being slow does not mean purposely dragging one's feet, rather it is being cautious and paying close attention to how things develop. We need to review, correct, and rethink our original plan and decisions in order to achieve success and perfection.

4. We should be wise in attaining difficult success. The wise win with strategy not physical strength, especially when our opponents have the advantage and there is seemingly no way to win. During the Period of the Warring States in China, there was a famous chariot race between a king and Tianji, a pupil of the famous strategist Sunzi. While the horses of Tianji were inferior in overall strength, Sunzi showed Tianji that by turning the rules of the games around – racing the slowest horse against the best one, the top against the mediocre, and the mediocre against the worst – the weak side overall could actually still win two to one. Thus, we need wisdom to win when the odds are against us.

The ancients said, "When our mind is clear as if resting in quiet and calm water, then there are no detestable issues in the world; when our thinking is balanced as if floating in a light and cool breeze, then there are no contemptible people under the sun." Chinese people tend to emphasize the cultivation of morals. We therefore need to remain calm and even-tempered, especially when we are dealing with people and issues. Through the cultivation of the mind, we can enhance tolerance so as to handle people and situations successfully.

Cause and Effect Between Self and Others

"People who respect others will always be respected." In human relationships, we need to treat others the way we want to be treated. As humans, we tend to reciprocate in whatever we do. Hence, if we treat others well, they will repay us with courtesy. On the contrary, if we are mean towards them, they will not show us kindness either. The cause and effect between self and others can guide us on how to conduct ourselves, and the following are some key considerations:

1. Humble people gain the respect of others. Being humble is one of the major ways we cultivate ourselves in life. It often happens that the more capable people are, the humbler they will be because they "learned to realize their own inadequacies." On the other hand, there are people who only scratch the surface and think they are really remarkable, believing they are truly learned and knowledgeable. As they show off their limited knowledge, they only end up being the empty bottles that make the most noise. In reality, it is easy to detect a person's depth because once they open their mouth, others will know right away. Truly knowledgeable people appreciate the virtue of humility, and others will respect them all the more. Those without substance try their best to cover up their insufficiencies, but end up only making themselves look even more callous. Therefore, in conducting ourselves we should be like wheat stalks heavy with grain, the more mature and ripe, the lower the heads go.

2. Boastful people instill doubt in the minds of others. Because they enjoy blowing their own horn, they are excessive in self-promotion and in showing off their

achievements. Consequently, they only generate doubt because one's praises should be sung by others, not one-self. For instance, if we are learned and ethical, our virtues will be known naturally by word of mouth, and so there is no need for us to say anything ourselves. Therefore, we should make demands of ourselves and be discreet, but never exaggerate in our self-promotion.

3. People who blame themselves gain the forgiveness of others. "Not all people are saints and sages, how can they be without faults? Correcting ourselves upon learning our mistakes is the greatest virtue." Sentient beings will inevitably make mistakes. When we err, we should repent and take the blame. With a sense of shame, we will certainly win the forgiveness of others. However, there are those who make mistakes and still argue and fight self-righteously, thinking their errors are a matter of course and so they should not be blamed. Their attitude will only gain the disdain of others, and it will be difficult for them to win forgiveness from anyone.

4. People who help themselves gain the support of others. It is said, "Heaven helps those who help themselves." Confucianism also teaches, "One must help oneself before others can offer assistance." If we want others to support us, we must first work hard ourselves. When we are strong enough to stand up on our own, make demands of ourselves, and have self-respect and humility, then naturally people around us will gladly support us in our achievements.

If we have all the advantages in everything we do, others will definitely be more inclined to take us to task. Therefore, the motto of Buddha's Light International Association is: " You are right and I am wrong; you are big and I am small; you have and I have not; you enjoy and I suffer." It is the best way in dealing with worldly matters and an important philosophy in getting along with people. Thus, we need to be mindful of the ways we can conduct ourselves in human relationships as described above.

Establishing Self and Others

In the past, Confucianists advocated that great men should better the world when in power; and they should better their own person when not in power. Likewise, Buddhism teaches the upholding of the Five Precepts and practicing the ten wholesome deeds as ways of establishing and enlightening self and others. The following are some keys for doing so:

1. Benevolence is being frugal with oneself while being generous with others. "It is difficult for a wealthy family to cultivate the Way; it is more difficult for a poor family to give alms." Truly benevolent people are those who can give their clothes and food away to those in need. Moreover, they are thrifty with themselves but generous in giving. They are committed to a life of simplicity and frugality but still give to the needy. Sharing what they have with other people signifies they are mindful of others. Such virtuous giving is how the benevolent conduct themselves.

2. Righteousness is being benevolent yet having few expectations. The wise and saintly take the initiative to practice kindness and compassion to help others without ulterior motives. "In giving, do not keep thinking about it; in receiving, do not forget about it" is a well-known motto. Buddhism teaches the "emptiness of the three aspects of giving" – the giver, the receiver, and the gift. We need to truly appreciate the emptiness of self and all phenomena with no desire for a repayment of good fortune. Furthermore, even if we are insulted or slandered, we can still be compassionate and not extinguish our desire to give. Giving without any expectation of being

repaid is a display of righteousness. The world today needs righteousness and the virtues of being selfless and generous.

3. Decorum is being personally righteous yet also passing it down through the family. Throughout history, decorum has been a core value of the Chinese people. Confucius said, "In life, treat one with civility, and in death, bury and make offerings to one with civility." It is more precious to pass down morals and righteousness to our future generations than give them money and property. Hence, societies would prefer morality and would settle for less money. Righteousness is the real treasure of a family, a nation, and one's life.

4. Wisdom is having civility yet also teaching our children. It is not enough to cultivate civility for ourselves alone. We need to teach our children and grandchildren the same, because the truly wise will instruct their offspring in the meaning of morals and righteousness. We often see people who uphold ethics and practice compassion, but they indulge their children with a life of dissipation. Consequently, no matter how good a reputation the parents have earned or how much wealth they have acquired, their legacy will only be ruined by the prodigal life of their children, which is sad indeed.

Mencius taught, "Benevolence is having the 'heart of mercy' to help others, and righteousness is having the 'heart of shame for unwholesomeness.' Decorum is having the 'heart of respect' or being respectful of others, and wisdom is having the 'heart of right and wrong' that can distinguish between them." Confucius and Mencius believed everyone could become a saint and a sage, and they are still admired and respected by so many people today. Likewise, the Buddha taught that every being could attain Buddhahood, because all sentient beings have Buddha nature. Therefore, on the journey of life, we should follow the examples of the wise and virtuous. We should become role models ourselves and go on to help others, so that we can establish both self and others.

Conditions for Establishing Ourselves

When airplanes fly, they follow a certain flight path, and trains traveling along the railway will stop at many stations on the rail-line set down for them. Likewise, ships follow shipping lanes that direct their course as they traverse the ocean. In life, we should also set goals and rely on them as markers, helping us to reach our destination safely.

To do so, we need certain conditions in order to establish ourselves. Sometimes, we may only think of ourselves and have no regard for others, making it difficult to find our place in human relationships. Other times we may be overly considerate of others and forget about our own position. When we put the cart before the horse, we will not be able to accomplish anything for ourselves or others. What are the conditions to establish ourselves? The following are some guidelines:

1. We need our own career. Having our own career or job does not necessarily mean establishing a factory or opening a store in order to make a lot of money. The ancients talked about the "three imperishables – one's virtues, one's achievements, and one's teachings." We can establish ourselves through writing that explains our philosophy and insights; we can also establish ourselves through service that society as a volunteer, social worker, Dharma teacher, or counselor. We can even establish ourselves through domestic chores, taking good care of our family members and teaching our children well. All these are ways to establish our career in life.

2. We need our own interests and hobbies. These represent food that nourishes our spirit. If we can cultivate the right interests and hobbies, it will be easier for us to

achieve a balance and find the middle path in life. For instance, music, art, travel, foreign languages, or research on special subjects are all good pursuits that can enrich our life. On the contrary, if we do not have wholesome interests, and indulge in drinking, gambling, substance abuse, or video games, we will only get into trouble. Worse still, we may commit many unwholesome deeds that we will regret later, since the welfare of our future would have certainly been jeopardized.

3. We need our own work. Within the Buddhist teaching of the Noble Eightfold Path, Right Livelihood entails engaging in appropriate work as a proper source of income. Work is nourishment for our spirit, and the fruit of our work gives us meaning and value in life. At the same time, we can grow and improve through the work we do. Unfortunately, some people choose to waste their precious time by either doing nothing all day long or engaging in unethical work, thus squandering life and achieving nothing. This is truly regrettable.

4. We need our own ethical standards. Ethics form the basis for a country's laws that maintain social order. They serve to protect society and provide security for its citizens. While there are social norms and principles that guide the public at large, we also need to observe our own discreet practices and guidelines. For instance, we can cherish what we have, make positive connections with others, serve and contribute to the community, and treat people with compassion. In addition, any altruistic intention we may have to help others in the Mahayana spirit of benefiting all sentient beings is the best medicine for curing our major diseases of anger and greed. Thus, we can purify our body and mind by enhancing our morality.

There are people who "stand on top of Mount Tai and look down on the world," while others "stand on their two feet and embrace the entire world in their hearts." Though we may be so poor that we cannot even find a place in life, as long as we are ready to work hard, we can still have the opportunity to be enriched in our lives. Confucius said, "One should not worry about not having a place to stand but be concerned with what one should stand on." In short, we should care more about the conditions we need to establish ourselves than contending a position in life.

Enhancing Our Morals

There are two major lessons in life: how to benefit others and how to enhance our morals. The following are a few guidelines on how to improve our morals:

1. When seeing others practice kind deeds, we need to praise them often. By doing so, we are expressing our recognition of their kindness. According to the Buddhist teachings, we should cultivate the merit of "taking sympathetic joy" in another's benevolence. As such, we should praise others when they speak well or perform good deeds. Generally speaking, we need to honor others for any deed that is worthy of praise. "With no anger from our mouth, we emit fragrance." When we praise others, we spread the light of compassion and wisdom. As we treat others kindly with positive speech, we make good connections and foster interpersonal relationships, and road to the future will become broader and smoother as more people welcome us wherever we go. Thus, we are actually giving ourselves the best service as well as a limitless treasure for our own benefit.

2. When others criticize us, we need to reflect more often. If others point out our shortcomings and mistakes, we need not explain too much in our own defense. Moreover, we should not retaliate with sharp words or a severe tone. Though we may not rejoice or make a bow of thanks on hearing about our faults, we must at least ask ourselves, "Have we really conducted ourselves in such a manner or have we really spoken such words?" When we reflect upon ourselves well, it will be easy to discover our mistakes so as to improve and make progress.

3. When hearing others' praise, we need to work even harder. Sometimes people may praise, encourage, or commend us. We should not be too pleased with ourselves and become complacent. We must never take the praise of others for granted. Instead, we should be even more aware of our shortcomings and reflect on them, being fully mindful of what is inadequate or lacking. Hence, we should work even harder than before, so that we can continue to strive for higher honors and achievements.

4. When hearing others slander us, we need to be vigilant. We should not get angry. When we accept criticism and slander as warnings with a heart of gratitude. By thanking others for the opportunity to repent, we are actually making progress with our morals.

People need to examine themselves all the time in order to enhance their morals and advance their practice. If our thinking and views can undergo a constant cycle of rebirth and revision, this will certainly enhance our morals.

How to Cultivate Our Morality

Since moral cultivation is the basis of interpersonal relationships, we need to cultivate our morality in order to strengthen ourselves so that we can better serve our friends, family, profession, society, and country. The following are some keys to cultivating our morality:

1. Frugality in our lifestyle. If we are greedy and vain, always indulging in sensual pleasures, we will inevitably engage in unwholesome deeds that may lead to the destruction of our family or even cost us our life. Li Shangyin, a famous poet of the Tang Dynasty, once noted, "The achievements of past sages, countries, and families teach us that success comes from frugality and failure from extravagance." However, frugality is not being miserly but rather practical without pretension. It is to be fully clothed without vanity, well-fed without gluttony, living simply in our daily life, and comfortable with our necessities. "It is hard to go from a luxurious life to a frugal one, but it is much easier the other way around" warned Sima Guang, a writer of the Song Dynasty. Regardless of our family fortune, if we have grown accustomed to excessive spending, poverty will be waiting for us just around the corner. By contrast, if we are prudent with our money and cherish what we have, then we can certainly accumulate savings over our lifetime. Therefore, frugality is the key to a better financial life.

2. Diligence in our career. We live in a society that abides by the law of evolution, where survival of the fittest is the norm. If we want to establish our career, we must

rely on our effort and diligence because if we only rely upon family support or influence, we are doomed to fail. "There is reward only in diligence, and nothing beneficial comes from indolence" according to an old Chinese saying.

Diligence can certainly improve our life, because it is the best remedy for the lack of talent. A person of humble origins is not necessarily destined for a life of poverty, because poverty can be overcome through hard work. If it were not for the sweat and unyielding determination of its founder, Kiichiro Toyoda, the Toyota Motor Company would not have become one of the world's largest manufacturers of automobiles today. Therefore, diligence is the key for establishing one's career.

3. Modesty in our relationships. Modesty is the secret to successful interpersonal relationships. No matter how educated we may be, we will not be highly regarded by our supervisor if we are arrogant. No matter how good looking some people are, they will never win praise if they are conceited. No matter how capable people are, friendships will forever elude them if they do not practice humility. "While modesty is the best way to avoid another's jealousy, respect is the best way to prevent another's insult," said Zeng Guofan, a general of the Qing Dynasty. In order for us to be well-liked and respected, we must be modest and humble in our manners. Therefore, modesty is the way to treat others.

4. Calmness in our conduct. "One can eliminate unfriendliness if one is cordial in receiving others," while getting angry is detrimental to one's health. Moreover, anger often drives us to make a mountain out of a molehill, transforming rational behavior into irrational outrages. It

is easy for us to make the wrong decision when we are angry. On the other hand, being calm and composed allows us to remain level-headed and reasonable. Equanimity is the best defense against stubbornness, irritability, and impatience. As an ancient sage once said, "Maintaining one's composure is the first step toward pacifying one's agitation, so one can calmly reduce large difficulties into small ones, and small ones into nothing." Therefore, we should exhibit calmness in whatever we do.

It is very dangerous to be unaware of our own mistakes and shortcomings. We should not just blame others for their mistakes and shortcomings. We should, instead, reflect on our own actions to see if they are right or wrong, good or bad, proper or improper. Moreover, it is important for us to remember that it is easier to deal with the external or material matters than internal ones. Likewise, it is easier to train our body than to discipline our mind, to get things done than to deal with people, and to read words than to understand their true meaning. The above four keys can serve as guidelines for cultivating ourselves morally.

Nurture Our Moral Character

To be considered human, people must possess moral character. Thus, it is important for us to enrich and cultivate our innate character on a daily basis. Qualities that distinguish us as humans are developed and established over a period of time with constant discipline and introspection. To nurture our moral character we must have an awareness of and commitment to living according to the following four truths:

1. Knowledge is the basis of modesty. We must be willing to learn if we want to nurture our character. By increasing our knowledge and understanding, our morals will be enhanced. As the saying goes, "A scholar well-versed in the classics is the perfect embodiment of virtue." Therefore, a learned person will better understand the virtues of modesty and temperance in displaying the superior quality of moral character.

2. Ignorance is the cause of arrogance. It is common for the uneducated or insecure to act conceited. They often flaunt their wealth by treating others with contempt and wield the sword of power so as to torment those who are weak. Thinking of themselves as courageous, they show off their bravado and indulge in their youthful energy. Regardless of their reason or how they choose to behave, they are nothing but the personification of ignorance, which is the primary cause of conceit. Therefore, those who are arrogant are, in fact, extremely deluded.

3. Humility is the root of dignity. Whether we are working or dealing with people, if we are humble in learning and

seeking advice, we will certainly improve ourselves. Hence, humility does not suggest submissiveness or an inferiority complex. Instead, it exhibits superior moral character. Therefore, a truly superior person acts with humility, and a truly humble person is one of unsurpassed virtue.

4. Conceit is the source of superficiality. Some people are overly confident and conceited. Lost in their own vanity, they assume they are better and wiser than others. They truly believe they are head and shoulders above everyone else in their abilities. However, such displays of egotism really demonstrate their sense of emptiness and insecurity, and only serves to expose their shallowness. In contrast, many people with high aspirations and ambition are reserved and humble, rarely boastful of their talents or knowledge. They appreciate the importance of concealing their abilities, biding time in conserving and strengthening their capabilities. Conceit, however, only makes a person shallower or more superficial.

A moral and noble character is the product of discipline and cultivation that are in step with the demands of the real world. It is unnecessary for us to be adorned with beautiful and expensive clothes, for they do not make us more virtuous. We should, instead, focus our attention on cultivating our character-nourishing ourselves with morality, dignifying ourselves with an unsurpassed sense of ethics and practice, and improving ourselves with humility. The nourishment of our character does not come from our appearance, position, or power. It is displayed in our demeanor, character, attitude and temperament. We should pay attention to these qualities in nurturing our moral character.

Four Imperatives to Enhancing Morals

Scholars want to increase their knowledge, while business professionals seek to realize their ambition. In cultivating our morals, we should also seek self-improvement over time. The following are keys for enhancing morals:

1. There is no greater peace than contentment. The best reward in life is peace, something that cannot be given to us by the Buddha or any God. We need to create the conditions and environment for peace within ourselves. The key to peace is contentment. When we are content with our position or rank in an organization, no one can obstruct us. If we are satisfied with the amount of financial wealth we have, then naturally, we will not be deluded by greed and ambition, or tempted to exploit others. Instead, we will gain peace.

2. There is no greater danger than speaking too much. According to the saying, "Mistakes are inevitable when too much is spoken." There are people who unwittingly say the wrong thing or leak a secret, and thus end up paying the price. This shows that there is no greater danger than speaking too much. The purpose of talking is mainly to share with others our thoughts and views. What we say should not only convey our intention, but also be considerate of the feelings and views of others. If we always speak inappropriately and hurt others in the process, it is best for us to remember that "silence is golden." At least, we should think before we speak, so that we can minimize the negative impact of our words.

3. There is nothing nobler than having no cravings. We do not need to always dress in beautiful garments, but should pay more attention to our inner cultivation. How can we nurture and beautify ourselves within with a noble character and moral cultivation? According to an old saying, "People gain a noble character naturally when they have no cravings." Some people are so greedy and keep craving for more that others scorn them. But if we exhibit self-respect and dignity in not being bound by cravings, our noble character and true nature will naturally shine.

4. There is nothing more base than lacking character. The ancients said, "Having no position does not mean we are low, but having no sense of shame makes us so." Our character hinges on how high our morals are. Some people may be rich and powerful, but they are scorned everywhere they go, because they lack moral cultivation. For instance, they may speak frivolously, conduct themselves improperly, or act with insatiable greed. When they undermine their own potential, others will not take them seriously. Hence, morals and character are the most beautiful and precious things in the world. When we lack ethics and a noble character, we are truly wretched.

We can cultivate a beautiful character and high morals through our daily life by being mindful of these four imperatives.

Monitoring Our Conduct

Humans are social animals, for we cannot live alone away from other people. As such, we will inevitably interact with others in our daily life. How to get along with people is therefore something we cannot afford to ignore. Confucius's admonition to "Check oneself with etiquette" means we should monitor our speech and action according to what is proper. In monitoring ourselves, we should control our behavior with ethics so that we will not violate others, and we must respect others by always upholding social mores. The following are guidelines on how to monitor ourselves:

1. It is best not to say anything we do not want others to hear. Speaking and listening to gossip are a part of human nature. We often hear people say, "I'll tell you a secret, but don't tell anyone!" But, you will hear the same secret from another person in no time. Furthermore, the one speaking will also hypocritically remind you, "I'll tell you, but don't let anyone know about this!" As we know, it is friends who most often inadvertently divulge each other's secrets. In the fable about the "King's Ear," we can appreciate that asking others to keep a secret is a difficult matter for both self and other. Therefore, if we do not want people to hear something, it is better not to say it.

2. It is best not to do anything we do not want others to know about. During the Eastern Han Dynasty, a minor official named Wang Mi liked to ingratiate his seniors. One time, he took a bag of gold to a senior official Yang Chun in the middle of the night and said, "It is late at night now and very dark. There are only the two of us

here, so please rest assured and accept this gift. No one will know about it." Yang was furious and admonished him saying, "Heaven knows, the earth knows, you know, and I know! How can nobody know?" Whenever we do something, it is impossible for no one to know about it. Therefore, it is best not to do anything we do not want others to know about.

3. It is best not to be too stern with those who may end up lying to us. *Humble Table, Wise Fare* reminds us, "Do not be too strict in admonishing the wrongs of others." If we want the people around us to give us honest advice and tell us the truth, we cannot be too strict in how we get along with them and dealing with situations, otherwise they will lie to protect themselves out of fear of being reprimanded. If we always give people a chance and provide them with appropriate support and care, they will tell us the truth in every matter. Therefore, if we do not want people to lie to us, it is best to be moderate in dealing with them.

4. It is best not to be too demanding on those who may end up indulging themselves. According to the saying, "In teaching others the right way, we should not be too demanding. The standard should be appropriate for them to follow." Some parents have very high expectations for their children. As a result, their aspirations become a heavy burden for the latter to bear. When that happens, the children will easily grow despondent and fall in with the wrong company. In general, in influencing others, a respectful attitude is needed in order to guide them toward benevolence. Otherwise, they will feel so oppressed that they will become like an over-pressed coil that loses its ability to spring back. If we do not want

others to become self-indulgent, we should not be too demanding.

Getting along with others is a major lesson in life. It affects the quality of our life in many important ways. If we know how to monitor our conduct, others will enjoy being with us, and we in turn can benefit from their friendship.

Integrity

Shakespeare once noted that true integrity becomes more evident through the hardships and tribulations of life. We can only mature in life through overcoming endless trials. According to a Chinese saying, one should "not be corrupted by wealth, moved by poverty, or subdued by power." Challenges come in the form of worldly possessions, love, and even loyalty. These all represent litmus tests for our integrity. On the journey of life, how can we uphold our integrity and not be distracted by external circumstances? The following are four metaphors that illustrate the meaning of integrity:

1. Gold can be polished without changing its color. Gold can withstand the tempering of very high temperatures and can be polished to a bright luster. It remains unchanged, and no external agent can ruin its original color. Since "genuine gold has no fear of tempering in the fire," it will not change its essence in high heat, thus, affecting its color. Similarly, the wise and virtuous will not alter their righteousness and integrity in face of external forces or temptations. Those who have the courage to meet the challenge will be like genuine gold that is tempered by the fire so as to eliminate all impurities. The process will not alter its color but only serves to make it purer.

2. Orchids can be transplanted without diminishing their fragrance. Orchids originally grow deep in the mountains, and yet their fragrance will not be muted even when they are transplanted into people's gardens. Therefore, the orchid has been used by scholars and poets over the centuries as metaphors for people of high prin-

ciples who do not seek fame or fortune. As Xunzi once asserted, such exemplars "quietly observe amidst the hustle bustle of life; strive to improve themselves through any difficulty." It illustrates how people with cultivation remain broad-minded in difficult times and respectful in fame and fortune. As Confucius put it, "One should worry about cultivation of the Way and not be concerned with being materially poor." People with high morals will not give up their passionate pursuit of the truth even when external circumstances change. They are people of true integrity.

3. Jade can be shattered without destroying its white luster. Even when a piece of white jade is broken into pieces, it still maintains its pure whiteness. The wise and ethical are like white jade, for temptations cannot change their morals and integrity, and insults cannot alter their resolve and ambition. The *Book of Rites* warns, "Don't be unscrupulous in money matters; don't shrink in face of hardship." The wise, therefore, do not alter their piety or morals.

4. Steel can be melted without reducing its strength. Iron and steel may be melted by fire, but its strength and hardness will not be changed. Confucius noted, "Armed forces may strip a commander-in-chief of his title; but even an ordinary man cannot be stripped of his resolve." In addition, "the wise and benevolent do not harm others in order to survive, but will sacrifice themselves for a just cause." Throughout Chinese history, there have been individuals of heroic spirit, who upheld their principles even in face of death. They were like steel that could be melted without reducing its strength.

The Song general Yue Fei once said, "Civil officials should not love money; military generals should be willing to die." We should never compromise our principles for fame and fortune, never lose our resolve because over the trials of poverty and insult, nor abandon our integrity in face of violence and power. We should maintain our color like gold, our fragrance like orchids, our purity like white jade, and our strength like steel.

Moral Resolve

What should we be afraid of? It should not be our lack of power or position but our lack of resolve. With fortitude we can overcome any adversity and hardship. We will be like a caterpillar breaking out of its cocoon to become a butterfly. However, people from privileged backgrounds sometimes show no resolve or aspiration. Often they do not appreciate their good causes and conditions and lose themselves in their good fortune. Therefore, it is imperative for us to have a strong sense of moral resolve, because it is a prerequisite for the cultivation of courage, determination, righteousness, and ethics. The following are some definitions of moral resolve:

1. We must have the resolve of character in poverty. Failure, success, good fortune, bad luck, gain, loss, honor, and disgrace are all facts of life. While it is very easy for some people to lose the will to fight when impoverished, others will not abandon their resolve even in the midst of destitution. The value of our character and fortitude lies beyond fame, fortune, and power. If a person is determined, poverty will become the motivation in enhancing their moral character. However, if a person is unwilling to make any improvement morally or intellectually, their character will remain inferior. If we wish to fortify and perfect our character, we must always be mindful of benevolence and humility in making positive connections with others.

2. We must show confidence and courage in danger. According to the Buddhist sutras, "When the state is in trouble, the three realms of existence are in chaos." Since the world is full of unknown variables, danger and

difficulty are impossible to avoid. Therefore, it is imperative for us to be confident and courageous; otherwise, we will be overcome by adversity and suffering. If we have no confidence in our future, how can we make progress and improve?

3. We must be kind and righteous in prosperity. It is easy for some people who have become rich overnight to forget their humble beginnings and spend lavishly. Their failure to be mindful of the past and cautious about their future will easily result in them losing everything they have gained. Therefore, we must appreciate the hardship of poverty when living in prosperity and have the good will and integrity to help the needy and unfortunate. By lending a helping hand without being obligated to do so, we enhance our moral character.

4. We must have the right intention and fortitude in cultivation. It does not matter what our faith is or what kind of practice we follow. What is important is for us to find purpose and strength in our cultivation. A Buddhist saying asserts, "If the cause is not right, the result will be perverse." If a person is not righteous, "even the truth will become a falsehood and the right Dharma will be corrupted." On the other hand, "a righteous person can transform deviant teachings into right ones." Therefore, it is imperative for us to be righteous in our cultivation as it will affect the attainment of moral fortitude. If our mind is weak and lacking in right intention, we will not have the mental strength to bring our cultivation into fruition.

People with moral resolve will be easily motivated by the feedback of others, regardless of whether it is positive or negative.

They will make the necessary improvements and progress accordingly. Furthermore, they will fully develop their potential under any type of circumstance, be it advantageous or disadvantageous. They are like the resilient bamboo shoots, moved by the howling wind and cold rain into producing a sprawling forest. In cultivating our moral resolve, we need to be aware of these lessons.

Cultivating Morals

Although we may be very wealthy, we do not necessarily live a happy life. We may be very learned, but we may not win friends. We may own many houses and businesses, but our days are not necessarily peaceful. Ultimately, it is best for us to have morals, because they are our best treasure. The following are keys to cultivating morals:

1. Do not blame others for small mistakes. Looking around the world, it is impossible for all the people we come across to be saints and sages. Thus, it is inevitable that they will make mistakes. We should not be too strict in reproaching others for their faults, especially minor ones. In conducting ourselves, we should blame ourselves as we would blame others, and forgive others as we would forgive ourselves. If we are able to refrain from blaming the small mistakes of others, we have reached the first stage of cultivating morals.

2. Do not disclose the secrets of others. In today's society, people value their privacy quite highly, and so we should not infringe on their right to privacy by disclosing the secrets of their private life. Members of the media should especially exercise professional restraint when it comes to personal information. As long as what they know will not cause the public any harm, they should have respect for the rights of others. According to the saying, "Publishing the kindness of others is repaying one's gratitude." Not disclosing the secrets of others, however, is cultivating one's ethics.

3. Do not keep thinking about the past transgressions of others. Most people will easily forget any major benefit they have received from others. However, if ever there are small mistakes and minor oversights on the part of others, they will complain and bicker, and tend to carry these minor grievances in their hearts all the time. People like that are quite small-minded. Since they themselves lack both magnanimity and virtue, they cannot tolerate others. Therefore, not harboring a grudge against others for old transgressions is a practice we should all follow.

4. Do not be jealous of benefits others enjoy. Some people are basically ill-willed. When they see others fail, they are happy; when others succeed or profit, they get upset. People like this do not want others to do well. As a result, they will find it difficult to make good friends, and they themselves will have problems gaining true happiness. Buddhism teaches us to experience "sympathetic joy," which means that we should not be jealous of the gains others enjoy, but instead, offer them our sincere blessing and be happy for them. Such is the merit of sympathetic joy, because with it we can cultivate our morals and also increase our merits.

We should all keep in mind the above four keys so that we can cultivate our morals.

The Beauty of Virtues

We all want to be someone outstanding, but in order to meet this goal, we need to have ability, wisdom, virtue and a good reputation. We especially need to uphold ethics and cultivate a good name. In cultivating our morals and paying attention to the beauty of virtues, we should keep the following definitions in mind:

1. Virtue is having no craving even in poverty. Some people may be poor, but they are not greedy and do not indulge in impractical pursuits or vanity. These are the ones who are rich at heart. "Seeking is not as good as not pursuing; retreating is superior to making an advance." Not seeking does not mean that we will end up with nothing. In fact, it is only those who are content do not crave for more. Hence, a virtuous person will feel content just to "enjoy" something instead of having to possess it. Such a person actually "owns" much more in the long run.

2. Virtue is giving to others in wealth. Which people are truly rich? They are not necessarily the ones with money. Some rich people have money, but they do not give or use it well. They become its slave and are actually poor, even though they are financially wealthy. On the other hand, people who are willing to give to others will gain much in return. Wealthy people who give are the truly rich. They are the ones who are rich in virtue.

3. Virtue is having respect for others even in high position. What are the criteria for nobility or high status? Holding

a high position does not ennoble anyone. Many officials in high positions enjoy great power but are despised and reviled by others. Are they the truly noble? On the other hand, there are humble people who treat others with integrity, care, and consideration all the time. Truly noble people do not look down on others from their high position. They are willing to help others solve problems and tolerate any unreasonable situation others may create. People with such tolerance are really noble.

4. Virtue is keeping one's integrity even while occupying a low status. Some people may come from poverty without any opportunities for success. However, they work hard and strive to progress in their own right. They do not latch onto power and wealth as the path to succeed. Moreover, they are courageous in expressing their righteous convictions and are not easily swayed by fear of rank or power. Such moral courage is stronger than brute authority in winning hearts and gaining respect.

In cultivating our virtues and improving our character, we need to be mindful of these definitions of virtue.

To Be Credible

Every Buddhist sutra begins with the phrase: "Thus I have heard" and closes with "receive the teachings with conviction and understanding, and then truly practice them." When the Buddhist scriptures were first compiled, Ananda, the attendant of the Buddha, recited all the teachings spoken by the Buddha that he heard. "Thus" means the Dharma according to what he himself had heard. "I have heard" is the assertion of the person believing what was said. "Receive the teachings with conviction and understanding, and then truly practice them" refers to the listeners accepting the Dharma the Buddha has taught and then practicing it.

The Buddha was able to convince his disciples to accept and believe what he taught, because he had attained perfect enlightenment. His myriad merits, perfect bearing, and perfection of the *six paramitas* were all models for his disciples. If we want others to believe and accept us, we must first establish a positive image and credibility before others will approve of us. When they are willing to follow us, they will accept and believe what we say. The following are some guidelines in how to gain the faith of others:

1. What we say and do should be consistent. It is important for us to be credible in our speech. When what we say and do match each other, we gain credibility. On the other hand, if we do not act the way we preach and fail to keep the promises we have made, we erode our trustworthiness, and others will look down on our character. Therefore, we must keep our promises and fulfill our tasks. People who speak and act the same will win the faith of others.

2. What we think and do should be consistent. Our behavior should reflect how we think, while our thoughts

should determine what we do. We should therefore not think one way and behave another. People will find it difficult to grasp what we are thinking if our actions differ from our thoughts, and they will not get close to us or trust us. Therefore, to be open about our intentions, our thoughts and actions must correspond. We should speak what we think, and never think one thing, while speaking and acting differently, otherwise our credibility will be greatly discounted by those around us.

3. What we do before and after a task should be consistent. In conducting ourselves, the worst mistake is to behave differently before and after any action in a way that is more convenient for us. People who behave like that usually show respect and act very serious before a matter is accomplished, but after it is done, they will change completely and may even start criticizing others. In time, others will see through such masks, so that even when their intentions are benevolent, others will not believe what they say anymore. Therefore, it is very important that we behave with consistency in the way we conduct ourselves.

4. How we deal with both large and small matters should be consistent. We must be fair and just. Equality is the truth of the universe, and we can only abide by the truth when we have a fair mind. Some people only want to do big things and look down on small matters. They will end up without success in anything they do. Others only want to take up small jobs and have no courage for taking up major undertakings. They in turn show no resolve. However, we must look at large and small things alike and treat them equally and fairly by applying the same principles. We need to be able to shoulder major respon-

sibilities, while not rejecting small matters. Thus, others will naturally trust us as we make a place for ourselves in this world.

How do we get others to trust us? We need compassion, sincerity, integrity, poise, and the resolve to shoulder major responsibilities. All these characteristics enable us to be credible and accepted by others.

Character Building

Saplings need water and fertilizer in order to grow, and children require nourishment so their young bodies and minds can develop well. Everything in life needs to be cultivated; our morals, knowledge, thinking, and more importantly, our character, all of these must be nurtured. The following are some guidelines for building character:

1. Clarity and justice nurture one's resolve. It is very important in life to be clear and just about matters. Everyone enjoys seeing a clear sky or a clean lake. Therefore, we need to cultivate clear thinking, conduct, and personality from a young age. Our resolve and ambition in life must be especially clear and just. Hence, from childhood we need to cultivate our resolve to assume major undertakings, speak the truth, and be noble. If we can continuously nurture our resolve and ambition, we can distance ourselves from impropriety, delusion, selfishness, and attachments. We will be able to constantly improve, expand, and elevate ourselves. Therefore, nurturing our resolve and ambition is essential to building character.

2. Awareness nurtures one's knowledge. Knowledge enriches us and enables us to reason well and see clearly the differences between right and wrong, good or bad. It is like a bright light that cuts through darkness, allowing us to prioritize properly and appreciate gains and losses. We can measure both our situation as well as that of others in order to better coexist. If we do not keep learning and enhancing our knowledge, others will not entrust us with major responsibilities. Hence, we must be always

aware of our own inadequacies and nurture our learning, courage, experience, and knowledge.

3. Resolve nurtures one's talents. Rice and vegetables both taste better when we allow the flavor to settle in for a while after they have been cooked. Like objects requiring maintenance after a period of time in order to last, our tired bodies also need rest to regain energy. Our talents as well need nurturing over time in order to improve. Hence, our abilities, enthusiasm, and ethics all need patient cultivation. In conducting ourselves and dealing with matters, we can never be indecisive, because no one likes an irresolute nature, nor should we always say yes to everything. We need determination in nurturing our skills and talents. When we can tell right from wrong, know how to prioritize, and assess good and bad, we will be better able to judge every situation and evaluate every matter clearly. Resolve nurtures and enhances our talents, allowing us to achieve success in whatever we do.

4. Magnanimity nurtures one's capacity. Whether we become a great person or accomplish major endeavors depends on our capacity. A withered branch can sprout and bloom again in the spring breeze, because resources and energy still reside within the dry twig. Many of Confucius's disciples were successful in their learning and cultivation of ethics, because they had great capacity. Therefore, besides our innate abilities, we also need broad knowledge and magnanimity. We must be considerate of others, give people space to develop, and provide opportunities for them from time to time. In our speech, we must be careful not to exaggerate or sound overbearing. When we are in positions of power over others, we

should not control them too much, because by leaving room and opportunity for others, we are actually benefiting ourselves.

Therefore, we need to pay attention to how to build our character with a clear sense of justice, awareness, resolve, and magnanimity.

How to Cultivate Deep Substance

When the ground is firm, it can support a heavy load; when the earth is solid, it can hold all things. In conducting ourselves and dealing with worldly matters, we must have substance and strength. Similarly, the foundation of society and the power of a nation also need to be deep and solid. The Confucian philosopher Xunzi once wrote, "The substance of benevolence is sufficient for settling a person; the sound of virtue is sufficient for transforming one." In Buddhism, cultivated masters and practitioners all relied on the depth and substance of their cultivation to accomplish their practice. For instance, Chan Master Puyuan carried water and cooked meals for thirty years at Mt. Nanchuan, and Master Hui Chong swept the grounds for forty years. When even masters like these had to cultivate their merit and conditions in this manner, how can ordinary people not do more to fortify themselves? The following are guidelines for how to cultivate deep substance:

1. Do not try to fly high when our wings are not fully-grown. The ancients taught that we should assess ourselves well before any endeavor. Are we are capable of carrying major responsibilities before we have matured? If not, we will only be derided as the "mantis trying to stop a cart with its arms." However, we must bear in mind some people may be late bloomers, while we should not rush to show off our talents nor give up too easily. As long as we are steadfast in our practice and can withstand the test of time, the day will come when we can spread our wings wide and soar high in the sky.

2. Do not act rashly in amending laws and rules that are not yet properly established. Laws provide people security and are guidelines for their conduct. When we conduct

matters according to the law, we can openly pursue what we need without upsetting the order. However, in amending any law or rule, we must give careful consideration and be mindful of the needs of the general public. Throughout Chinese history, there were occasions when new laws were established that faced strong opposition or created too many enemies. Those who imposed such laws ended up being overthrown. Therefore, before the conditions are right for any new law or rule to be established and receive universal acceptance, we should never act rashly. Otherwise, we will only gain the rejection of the general public.

3. Do not try to exhibit ourselves if our morals and virtues are still shallow. Morals and ethics are developed on the right path by benefiting others, and to be complete in morals and ethics is precious to humanity. If our cultivation of morals and ethics is incomplete, it is easy for us to expose our callousness when we interact with other people. In time, they will not want to open their heart to us. Likewise, if we lack character and morals, our coworkers will not want to listen to us, and casual acquaintances will not trust us either. Therefore, the wise of old will refrain from trying to "speak profoundly with acquaintances."

4. Do not take up major responsibility when our knowledge is incomplete. "If one's practice is deep, even an iron pestle can be reduced to a needle." We must go deep into any matter we are learning or studying, before we can proceed to make a plan and strategy for achieving our goals. By taking these steps, we will be able accomplish our goals much faster and easier. On the other hand, when our knowledge and ability are not yet complete, we

should not act rashly by taking up a major responsibility. When our learning is inadequate and our dreams inflated, we can set ourselves up with unrealistic expectations, for we say and do would just be like building castles in the air. Hence, we should not take up major responsibilities if our knowledge is incomplete.

We should not casually pick fruit when they are not ripe. Similarly, when hens hatch eggs, they do not peck at them when the time is not right. A skyscraper starts from the ground, and success in our endeavors also requires us to take one step at a time before we are able to grow steadily. We should never ignore the importance of how to cultivate deep substance.

Four Stages in Life

Just as the year goes through its seasons, life goes through the stages of birth, aging, sickness, and death as people transmigrate through the cycle of living and dying. Within our lifetime, the "four stages" are childhood, youth, maturity, and old age. How do we plan and develop our life within these four stages? The following are some guidelines:

1. Be open and ambitious in childhood. The Daoist sage Laozi said, "An old tree grows from a sapling, a nine story pagoda begins with pile of dirt, a journey of a thousand miles starts with a single step." Childhood is the beginning of life and the first step toward cultivating ambition and ability towards a bright future. The Song dynasty scholar Fan Zongyen vowed to "Be anxious of the world's worries before they arise; and partake in the world's joy after it has been established." If we are able to emulate the spirit of the wise and virtuous, our life will certainly rise to a higher level.

2. Be resilient and hard-working in our youth. When we are young, we should not focus on enjoying the fruits of those who came before us, squandering the inheritance our parents bequeathed on us. "We reap what we sow!" Without the sweat of our labors, we will not be able to gain a bountiful harvest. Without laboring and giving our heart, we will not taste the sweetness of success. Hence, we all need to make good use of our youthful days to strive on in life. We must be ready to accept hardships in order to survive and forge our career.

3. Do not underestimate ourselves in our mature years. The famous modern scholar Hu Shi once said, "What I am today is the result of everything that has taken place in the past. There is no need to think too much or be sad over it." By the time we reach middle age, we sometimes look back in life or try to foresee the future. We may bemoan the fact that we have lived nearly half a century and not been able to achieve many accomplishments, merely living life in vain. In reality, middle age is the golden age in life because we have matured. As Dr. Sun Yat-sen asserted, "Resolve to accomplish major undertakings, not to simply covet a title." Even though we may be doing seemingly minor jobs, we still have to do them well. For instance, if we drive a cab, we drive it so well that every passenger is happy riding with us. If we are a minor construction worker, we also put our heart into ensuring that people will feel safe in the buildings we are constructing. Janitors often risk their own health in ensuring a clean environment. They have no fear of the dirt and odor because they are contributing toward the world's well being. Hence, we should not underestimate ourselves in middle age.

4. Pass on our experience in old age. An old horse knows the way, while an old cow can best care for the calf. It is commonly accepted in Asian culture that senior citizens are a family's treasure. When we reach old age, we realize that the meaning of life no longer lies in our physical body but in the limitless life of our merit and wisdom. Elderly people are rich in life's experiences. Old age is the time for them to pass on their wisdom and knowledge. "New branches come from an old trunk," and so life is passed on to future generations.

When the four elements that make up our physical body

are in harmony, we will live in ease, good health, and high spirits. When we live according to the "four right kinds of diligence," we can distance ourselves from worries as we cultivate ourselves through continuous practice. As such, all sentient beings will prosper when they live according to the cycle of the four seasons. *The Commentary on the Spring and Autumn Annals* states, "The wise work in four phases of the day: listen to reports in the morning, visit during the day, make changes in the evening, and rest at night." This quotation is an illustration of planning for the different parts of the day. Similarly, each of the four stages of life comes with its own responsibility and each is worthy of our learning and hard work.

Four Keys in Life

We all wish to gain some reward, some measure of peace and prosperity in life. But how do we fulfill our wishes? The following are some guidelines:

1. We need to make good neighbors. "One needs good neighbors at home and good companions during travel." When we have good neighbors, we can live in peace. The mother of Mencius moved their home three times when he was a child. She did this in order to find a positive environment in which her son could study and learn well, so that he could be inspired by kindness and beauty and cultivate a noble character. Nowadays, parents also look for good communities in which to live for the sake of their children. Since we appreciate the importance of good neighbors, we ourselves need to act neighborly as well.

2. We need to befriend good people. Friends play a very important role in our life, so making the right friends is a major lesson we must learn. Confucius taught that "Friends should be righteous, forgiving, and knowledgeable." Likewise, we should make friends with people who are honest, upright, learned, and ethical. We should also look for kindness and integrity. Friends should support and encourage one another by counseling each other, in order to change one's errant ways and advance towards goodness. Friends should especially tolerate each other's unintentional mistakes and not bicker or calculate over trivial matters. Friends with these qualities are truly valuable.

3. We need to read good books. Books are like people; there are good ones and there are bad ones. In the past, people used to say, "Reading is beneficial." However, nowadays we see so many publications that sell gossip and profanity. Reading them brings us no benefit whatsoever, because they will only lead us down the wrong path. This is why we must choose good books to read. The best choices are inspirational books that can help us grow in wisdom and enhance our morals and knowledge.

4. We need to do good deeds. We have to make use of our limited lifespan to create value in our life and pursue everlasting spirituality. Thus, we need to do as many good deeds as possible on a regular basis. We have to apply our best effort to any cause that benefits society, the country, and humanity. We should realize the energy of life through work and service, and in the process, we will not only benefit others, but also help ourselves as well.

Ultimately, in order to fulfill our own wishes, we need to first be mindful of these four keys in life.

Life's Four Virtues

Humans should not be without virtue, and there are four kinds of virtue in particular that must be cultivated during our lifetime. They are as follows:

1. The source of wisdom lies in a tranquil mind. We all hope to be smart and wise. But how do we do so? "When there is stillness, there is tranquility; when there is tranquility, there is consideration; and when there is consideration, there is accomplishment," said *The Great Learning*. The spring of wisdom, thus, has its source within the calm mind. A tranquil mind is like muddy water that has settled and can reflect light clearly. Accordingly, everyone should set aside at least one hour of quiet time a day or three hours a week for introspection and planning. Since tranquility is the source of wisdom, Zhu Geliang, noted for his great wisdom, constantly reminded himself with the following motto: "In leading a quiet life, one can accomplish something lasting."

2. The capacity for forbearance lies in a compassionate mind. How do we show our love for others and kindness to the world? We need to have compassion if we want to eradicate suffering, provide happiness, treat everyone as an equal, and walk in others' shoes. When the Buddha was still practicing as a bodhisattva in a previous life, he was full of loving-kindness that enabled him to feel for all living beings. It even allowed him to feed a piece of his flesh to an eagle and offer his whole body to a tiger. Avalokitesvara Bodhisattva also responded to the suffering of sentient beings by manifesting in thirty-three forms to save people according to their needs. As the

embodiment of great loving-kindness and compassion, the bodhisattva shows that the capacity for forbearance ultimately lies within a compassionate mind.

3. The act of courage lies in an unbending will. Since the beginning of time, adversity has been overcome by a firm resolve which enables survivors to conquer the most dangerous conditions or the physically challenged to overcome their disabilities. Galileo once said, "Real life is like a burning furnace where metals are refined to make fine steel; whatever cannot withstand the heat becomes mere scrap metal." If we want to pass the rigorous test of the burning furnace in real life, we must be firm in our resolve by facing every challenge with courage and every obstacle without fear. Therefore, the act of courage lies in a will that is firm and unyielding.

4. The actualization of our vow lies in making selfless contributions. "Heaven is without bias in its protection, the earth is without prejudice in its support, and the sun and the moon are without favor in their illumination," said Confucius. Heaven, earth, the moon, and the sun are selfless in fulfilling their individual greatness. If we want to accomplish something, we must rely on the power of selfless vows, like those made by Amitabha Buddha, who had made forty-eight great vows to deliver all beings while he was a monk named "Dharma-Treasure." Because of the power of his vows, Amitabha Buddha was able to establish the most dignified Pure Land of ultimate bliss. Similarly, Ksitigarbha Bodhisattva was able to fulfill the fruit of the way because of his great vow to liberate infinite numbers of beings. We can also resolve to be good and virtuous, to build bridges and pave roads for the sake of all beings, and to be a person of knowl-

edge so we can use what we have learned to benefit society and everyone within. In this regard, the actualization of our vow lies in making selfless contributions.

Life is like a marathon where virtues are deeply cultivated to endure and last. If we want to smoothly overcome every crisis on the journey of life, we must cultivate the above four virtues.

Life's True reality

People often ask, "Where do we come from? Where do we go after death?" When the Buddha renounced his life as a layperson, his aim was to discover the truth about life and the reality of birth, old age, sickness, and death. What then is the ultimate reality of life? The following four points offer an explanation:

1. Realize that the physical body is impermanent; it is like a dream or an illusion. The "bubble" was used as an analogy in the *Nirvana Sutra* to describe the vulnerability of the human body, which can be extinguished in an instant because it is only made from the four elements of earth, water, fire and wind. Furthermore, our body undergoes changes at each stage from birth, childhood, adolescence, adulthood to old age. The Buddhist scriptures have likened it to the frailty of a plantain tree. Sickness will trouble us when the four elements are not in harmony, and death will take us when the elements are no longer held together as a whole. As such, the physical body is impermanent like a dream or an illusion.

2. Realize that life is not infinite; it is like a bubble or a shadow. Where is life after decades of living? Where is life when the body is sick and old? Where is life when death finally comes to us? Samantabhadra Bodhisattva's *Exhortation to the Masses* warns us, "with each passing day, our life becomes shorter." Even for those of us whose life really begins at seventy and can live until the age of one hundred and twenty, yet ultimately, no one can escape old age, sickness and death. In a famous poem, Cao Cao of the Wei Kingdom once compared life's duration to morning dew that will evaporate when the sun

rises. Life is like a bubble that will burst when blown upon or a shadow that will disappear when it enters darkness. Therefore, life is everything but enduring; it is like a bubble or shadow.

3. Realize that wealth is insubstantial; it is like dewdrops or lightning. "Amidst a thousand palaces, a night's sleep requires only eight feet of space; out of ten thousand acres of grain, how much is needed for a day's meal?" Although it is everyone's wish to have as much wealth as the world can possibly offer, how much money can one honestly spend? *The Treatise on the Perfection of Great Wisdom* reminds us that wealth is susceptible to these effects–thieves committing robberies; corrupt officials taking bribes; the prodigal child squandering the family fortune; and water, fire and war destroying property. As such, wealth is as insubstantial as drops of dew or flashes of lightning.

4. Realize that achievements are empty; they are like frost and snow. Although it is common for all the world's people to relentlessly pursue fame and fortune, they have failed to realize their true nature – wealth, status and laurels are not real. When a person is in a position of power, he or she will have no problem making a lot of friends, but once they have fallen out of favor, friends will be hard to come by. Therefore, accomplishments are nothing but frost and snow that instantly melt when the sun shines.

Life indeed is impermanent, unsatisfactory, empty, and without a self-nature. If we want to seek a true self that is beyond grasping and attachment, we must see life as it really is, without delusion or pretense in accordance with the above.

Four Gains in Life

People all want to gain something in life. They seek money, love, material goods or other kinds of benefit. Moreover, they often desire whatever they can see or dream of. The truth is, we stand a chance of losing whatever we gain. This is especially true because what is really worth gaining is not necessarily tangible. Rulers of a country seek the affection of the citizenry and leaders in senior positions look for the support of subordinates. These are real and worthy gains in life, and the following are some approaches towards worthy gains in life:

1. Humility gains respect. In getting along with others, we will certainly gain their respect if we are humble and respectful. "Those who respect others will always be well-respected; those who love others will always be well-loved." When we are humble and respectful towards others, they will reciprocate. According to the saying, "By being diligent and humble, one can count on many for support; by being arrogant and conceited, one can count on being promptly abandoned by others." So how do we bridge the distance between self and others, and how can we win the support of the general public? The best way is to be a little more deferential and show a little more respect.

2. Magnanimity gains support. The Tang Dynasty official Liu Zongyuan loved his subjects so much that they later built a special shrine in his honor to show their gratitude. If we can treat others with magnanimity, we can gain their support. But on the contrary, we will only win their disdain if we are harsh and strict. Over the centuries, there have been many incidents where ordinary citizens

revolted against their government. The reasons were mostly due to tyrannical officials levying heavy taxes, and thus, making life insufferable for their people. Naturally, the subjects were compelled to rebel. Hence, "only magnanimity can carry people and only generosity can bear heavy tasks." If we want to gain the support of others, magnanimity is a virtue we must have.

3. Integrity gains trust. The story of the King You of the Zhou dynasty deceiving his ministers with false alarms in order to please his favorite concubine has been a lesson for Chinese people throughout the ages. How do we gain the trust of others in our daily life? In dealing with people, we must ensure them of our honesty by keeping our verbal promises. Furthermore, we need to conduct ourselves with propriety; only then will others trust us. During the Spring and Autumn Period, the integrity of Zheng Le from the State of Lu symbolized the trust of his country, so that contemporaries would comment: "upon seeing his sincerity, even rocks will open up." The Qing Dynasty minister Zeng Guofan once famously asserted, "With sincerity even gold and rock can be penetrated." Trust and honesty are indeed invaluable treasures that are indispensable to life.

4. Compassion gains nobility. We often describe wise rulers as being "benevolent to their citizens and loving towards their subjects." Similarly, buddhas and bodhisattvas are described as "protecting sentient beings with compassion," and "having compassion for those with no connection to them, and loving-kindness to those sharing the same existence." They all remind us that we need a virtuous heart and a compassionate mind in order to gain the respect of others. Moreover, treating people

with compassion and generosity not only wins their admiration, but also enhances our own morals. This is what we mean by "compassion gains nobility."

"Respect brings no insult, while magnanimity gains support. In winning the trust of others, integrity is important, and compassion inspires others." If we want to make true gains in life, we should follow these approaches.

Four Joys in Life

Life can feel like the four seasons, and so can our state of mind. If we are trapped in sorrow and pain, then even though it may be springtime, it will feel like the coldness of winter. If our mind is liberated from the bondage of trouble, we will feel cool and easy even in the middle of summer. Therefore, when we are able to transcend the hot and cold of human sentiments, each of the four seasons will be filled with endless delight. The following are some ways to enjoy each season:

1. Marvel at the fragrant blossoms in spring. When spring arrives, the earth awakens, and flowers bloom in all their glory of their colors. They are elegant and beautiful, spreading bouquets of perfume. Spring is like a newborn baby full of life and energy. Wherever spring goes, life is filled with hope. "Green grass and fragrant flowers, travelers truly delight in them." Life is certainly enjoyable at this time.

2. Enjoy a taste of sweet tea in summer. If summer feels too hot for you, share a cup of tea with a few good friends in a gazebo or under the shade of a tree. It would feel like drinking sweet dew. When friends gather, the friendly exchange and camaraderie are like gentle breezes. Summer! Just take time to sip some tea and savor its flavor as our heart warms up. It is certainly a joyful time in life.

3. Admire the cool moon in autumn. "The moon is particularly bright by mid-autumn." Autumn is the season when we get closer to the bright and clear moon. Once

the weather gets cool, the moon in the sky appears even cooler and brighter. When admiring the white shining moon, we may be reminded of what Master Han Shan once said, "My heart is like the autumn moon, its reflection clear and white in the blue water. There is nothing that can compare; what more can I say?" Tang Dynasty Li Bai expressed a similar carefree and romantic feeling in the following lines: "I raise my glass to invite the moon, forming a company of three along with my shadow." Viewing a full autumn moon is another joy in life.

4. Listen to the firecrackers in winter. When winter comes, the New Year arrives. Households set off firecrackers to bring good fortune for the new year which can be heard everywhere. The distance between people becomes so much closer: "The old year leaves with the sound of firecrackers. Like everything else, new scrolls of blessings replace old ones on walls." A new year allows us to start everything anew, bringing a renewal of hope.

Spring, summer, autumn, and winter, each has its own vista and beauty. Likewise, the twenty-four hours in the day are also full of joy. Aren't we happy putting on clothes, eating a delicious meal, or going out for a ride to admire the scenery? We can also be at peace while walking or exercising. Therefore, we should be looking for happiness in our daily activities, for there is no need to become mired in sorrow and suffering. Why not seek out the joys of life every season of the year?

Four Failures in Life

We all enjoy the taste of success because it is self-affirming and gives us confidence, hope, and a sense of accomplishment and honor. On the other hand, nobody likes failure because it spells setback, remorse, pain, and embarrassment. There are causes and conditions behind both success and failure. The following are some reasons for failures in life:

1. Those who are muddled and contemptuous in leading others without ability will fail. If people heading an organization are muddled and incapable and do not conduct themselves within reason, the law, and human feelings, their subordinates will certainly resent working for them. Thus, they will naturally fail. When Marie Antoinette said, "Let them eat cake," she became the object of derision over the ages. It is not hard to imagine the reason behind the subsequent fall of the French monarchy.

2. Those who are selfish and arrogant without regard for others will fail. "Selfishness inevitably breeds trouble." In Chinese history, when the Han and the Chu were fighting for the empire, the Chu leader, Xiang Yu, was jealous of the wise and virtuous. He did not give credit where it was due nor offer a share in any benefit. His generals and soldiers eventually lost faith, and in the end his bid for ruling the land was destroyed. As the saying goes, "Those who respect others will be well respected." Selfish people have no one in their hearts. Worse still, they claim credit and deny all faults, for they only keep benefits for themselves and push their responsibilities onto someone else. How can people like that win any

respect? How can they not fail?

3. Those who are undisciplined and uncouth without regard for law and decorum will fail. "Without a ruler or compass, one cannot make a square or circle; without a level, one cannot rectify a slant." Laws and rules for decorum are the compass and level in life that everyone must follow. These are the keys to maintaining order. Some people have no regard for law and order, and they test the law with what they do and only end up putting themselves in imminent danger. Convicted criminals lose their freedom because they have violated the law. For law-abiding citizens, even though they may not be making much profit, will not welcome undue peril, and so life for them will naturally be smoother.

4. Those who are inconsistent and deceitful without credibility will fail. It is said in the *Commentary on the Spring and Autumn Annals*, "The wise have respect for others, and, thus, earn their credibility." If we overlook our reputation and pay no attention to our agreements, frequently failing to keep our promises and taking advantage of others, then how can we ever gain their trust? Lu Bu from the Eastern Han Dynasty was a fierce warrior who waged battles and won victories everywhere he went. He was famous for single-handedly fighting with three renowned generals of the time and was considered supreme in the martial arts of his era. However, he was inconsistent in character and lacked credibility in what he did. In the end, his subordinates revolted against him, and as a consequence, he was captured and killed by his enemies. Similarly, if we lack credibility and trust, we will certainly fail.

We should have no fear of failure but only of falling down and being unable to get up again. Moreover, we should not be fearful of admitting our mistakes nor knowing the reasons for our failure. We should contemplate on the above four causes and conditions behind failure and remain ever mindful of them.

Finding the Way, Morals, and Fortune in Life

We all wish for the right path, moral virtues and good fortune in life. None of these are gained by merely wishing for them; we need to know how we to cultivate them. The following are some guidelines for doing so:

1. The Way is attained through tranquility. Where can we find the Way? It resides in the world of tranquility. If we can quiet our body and mind, the Way will manifest itself naturally. The Way is just and universal. It can be shared by everyone and will not change over time. However, if we fail to calm our body and mind, or rid ourselves of deluded thoughts that agitate us physically and mentally, we will find it difficult to attain the Way.

2. Morals are born by overcoming our desires. What are morals? These are the standards we set for ourselves, but do not involve making demands upon others. We often unconsciously blame people and circumstances around us—either that person is wrong or this thing is bad. However, people with morals will not conduct themselves in this manner. They will only make demands on themselves in an attempt to improve their own character and fulfill what they have set out to do.

3. Good fortune is gained through frugality in daily life. We must cherish what we have in order to gain better fortune. On the other hand, if we are wasteful and squander all our good fortune, then naturally, we will have nothing left. Hence, it is better for us to cultivate good fortune with diligence and simplicity.

4. Life is sustained with harmony. Buddhism teaches us
   that the four elements that make up our physical body
   and all phenomena in the world are empty. It also
   reminds us to employ the impermanent life we have to
   cultivate the truth. We must have "life" in order to exist
   in the world. When our life ends, our body will no
   longer belong to us. Without a physical body, we have
   no being to speak of. Therefore, we need to care for our
   body in order to sustain life. Harmony and a smooth flow
   of all elements are fundamental for life to go on. Our
   energy, mind, and nature must be in harmonious synergy
   in order for life to sustain itself.

How do we gain the Way, cultivate morals, good fortune,
and a good life? We need to be mindful of the above if we want to
realize our goals.

How to Manage Ourselves

People today emphasize planning, organization, and management in whatever they pursue. Our career, family, and human relationships all need management. Moreover, the wise put the "management" culture above social benefit, the benevolent put righteousness above charity, the courteous put benevolent friends above wealth, and practitioners put Dharma joy above happiness. The truth is that each person needs to know how to manage themselves, the keys of which are as follows.

1. In the realm of learning, diligently pursue the essence of knowledge. Life is one of endless cycle of learning. According to the saying, "Learning is never complete, even if we live to an old age." Learning is not for the moment, for it is a life-long pursuit. Moreover, it is not limited to schools. There are many subjects to learn within a household, company, community, or an entire society. All of them are like a university that provides us with numerous topics, none of which can be exhausted even through a lifetime of effort. In pursuing any topic, it is most important to seek its essence, for there is always room for improvement. In order to raise ourselves to a higher level, we should always strive to improve, instead of becoming complacent or too self-assured.

2. In the realm of commerce, broadly expand one's connections. Ours is an age of advanced information exchange and active industrial and commercial development. We all need to join the workforce after graduating from school. Whether it is in commerce, industry or agriculture, there are various associations, unions or co-ops from which we can choose. These are illustrations of the

modern age in which teamwork and human interaction are emphasized. When we participate in any meeting related to our work, we need to pay attention to the relationships on both the horizontal and vertical planes, and we should constantly seek to expand our social circle. When we can appreciate multi-level human relationships, we will be able to go broad and deep, and succeed much more easily in what we do.

3. In the realm of human relationships, cultivate a good sense of humor. No individual is an island, and no one can live in isolation, especially in today's society where human interaction is inevitable and pervasive. People nowadays are closely linked to their community, the world, and even the universe. For this reason, we really need to know how to manage human relationships well. We have to offer others joy and benefit. In developing our career, we must be cheerful and able to share a laugh with others. Therefore, in order to gain the support of others, we need to have a good sense of humor and not be too stiff or austere.

4. In the realm of solitude, maintain a mind of equanimity. Keeping busy and feeling tense is often the portrait of the modern lifestyle. But when we are alone by ourselves at night after a day of hustle and bustle at the workplace, we should not be dwelling over what went right or wrong during the day between self and others. We should not be obsessing on good and bad or loss and gain experienced at work. Instead, we should calm ourselves down and enjoy the peace and quiet of our spiritual world, in order to gain the strength required to start the next day refreshed.

The famed "god of management" Konosuke Matsushita accomplished phenomenal success in his career. However, it was his humanistic "paternal management" that earned him the title and his great accomplishment. Therefore, in conducting ourselves, not only do we need to manage our tangible wealth well, but more importantly, we also have to manage the intangible world of our spirit, because this is the key to good self-management.

Strengthening Ourselves

Birds gather where trees are lush and green, and fish breed where the ocean is deep and wide. As humans, we must first strengthen ourselves before we can provide others with shelter. Some people are physically fit but are unwell in their mind. They are not as healthy as those who are physically disabled but have a positive attitude in life. In strengthening ourselves, we need adopt the following guidelines regarding our thinking and mental outlook:

1. It is more important to have morals than money. Most people wish for financial success. However, money does not necessarily solve one's problems, and rich people are not always happy. When we consider historic figures like Mahatma Gandhi or Sir Thomas More, both of whom lived very difficult lives, we can appreciate them as great men with ethics and principles. On the other hand, if we consider a Nero or Hitler, we will recognize both rulers as immoral. We can see from this that someone with morals can live forever in people's hearts. Therefore, ethics and morals are far superior to money and power.

2. It is better to be content than to have fame and fortune. Many rich and powerful people in the world are not necessarily content with their lot. They may not know how to make good use of their wealth or be very greedy, seeking endlessly for more. They may be rich in wealth but poor in reality. Some people may be penniless, but their days are filled with joy and contentment, because they can see the beauty of the world. Even though they do not possess any riches, they live a rich life. Therefore, joy and contentment constitute the greatest wealth in life.

3. It is better to help ourselves than seek it from others. According to the saying, "While it is difficult to rise to heaven, it is even harder to seek help from others." When we have to ask for help from others on every matter, life is certainly difficult. Someone once asked, "Why does Guayin Bodhisattva hold a string of beads in her hand? What is she reciting?" The answer is, "She is reciting the reciting the name Guanyin." Why does Guanyin recite her own name?" Because it is better to help oneself than to ask others for assistance. That is why we have to train, strengthen, and be responsible for ourselves.

4. It is better to motivate ourselves than to lose our spirit. Many people, when faced with setbacks and hardships, give up on what they had set out to do. Worse still, they lose their drive and spirit as they slip into the pit of despair. People like this will never succeed in life because they must realize that "without going through bone-chilling cold, the plum blossoms will not emit their fragrance." The more it rains on us, the more we should strive; the more difficult the times, the more we should rise to the occasion with spirit. After all, "failure is the mother of success." When we are able to learn from the experience of our setbacks, we will surely succeed one day.

Therefore, in strengthening ourselves in life, we should be mindful of the above.

Delivering Ourselves

Buddhism speaks of deliverance through reciting the Buddhist scriptures. Daoism speaks of the same through its rituals, while Christianity affirms deliverance through prayer. Every religion wants people to gain deliverance. Yet, we do not need to pray for the deliverance of our ancestors or dead spirits. Delivering ourselves and others in this life is much more important. The following are some guidelines for doing so:

1. Delivering our enemies creates broad and positive connections. A Ming scholar once said, "Matters rise endlessly without ceasing; people harm one another continuously without stopping. It is better to resolve grudges with old enemies than making new ones. Just turn around to see where we are heading." People all look for world peace, but there are still endless battles going on. Families all seek harmony, but domestic violence never seems to cease. These are the consequence of people treating each other as enemies. Therefore, in the pursuit of universal harmony and peace among human beings, we should treat everyone equally with no distinction between friend or foe. By coexisting in peace, we can truly create broad connections with others.

2. Delivering ourselves from delusions gains enlightenment. When deluded thoughts cloud our mind, it is very difficult to see the reality of any matter. If delusions were to cease, then the clear enlightenment within us will naturally manifest. It is like stirring up muddy waters. The more we stir, the muddier the water gets. Once we stop stirring, the mud and dirt will sink to the bottom and clear water will appear.

3. Delivering ourselves from sorrow brings peace. If we are always worried and sad, our body and mind will be out of balance. As Confucius pointed out, "Something we don't have, we worry about not getting; something we do have, we worry about losing." We are always living anxiously between gain and loss, creating endless worries for ourselves. In order to gain peace, we need to transform sorrow into joy. By letting go of sorrow, we will gain happiness.

4. Delivering ourselves allows us to gain liberation. There are many reasons why we do not receive deliverance. Mainly, it is due to our never-ending greed, anger, and delusion. We have too many worries and troubles concerning friends and enemies, which consistently give rise to confused and rambling thoughts in our minds. If we are able to transcend all the worries and ignorance in our mind, we can gain generosity, joy, compassion, brightness, equality, peace, enlightenment, and liberation. How wonderful life it would be!

Hence, if we want to deliver ourselves, we first need to achieve the above.

Self-Reflection

Most people tend to scrutinize others with their eyes, constantly trying to assess who is good, who is bad, or who is right and who is wrong. In reality, the most important thing in life is not to scrutinize the behavior and attributes of others but to examine oneself. The following are some keys to self-reflection:

1. Awareness of danger in high places can make us humble and safe. Some people hold high positions and believe they can look down on the rest of the world from their perch. Thus, they fire off orders at others and abuse all the power they can muster. In reality, the higher the position they hold, the more they should appreciate the adage "It is more lonely on the mountain-top." If they fail to appreciate humility and self-cultivation, they may even find themselves in imminent danger. Therefore, if people in high places are aware of their precarious positions, they will treat others with humility. Moreover, they need to keep examining themselves and improving, while at the same time making more demands on themselves.

2. Fear of overflowing capacity can allow us to absorb all streams and rivers like the ocean. "Arrogance brings harm; humility produces benefits." If we are arrogant, we are like water in a cup that overflows when full, because we will not be able to expand like rivers or oceans. Therefore, we need to be humble. We should be like the ocean absorbing and embracing hundreds of streams and rivers, or the high mountain that does not reject any dirt or pebble. If we can defer to others regardless of rank or status, and be able to ask them for help and advice, not only can we win their friendship, but we will

also be able to accomplish tasks with many more supporting conditions.

3. Sharing wealth can help us enjoy our prosperity while
helping the needy. In enjoying the fame and fortune
earned through our diligence and the merits of our positive causes and conditions, we must realize that the world
is impermanent. Since everything arises from certain
causes and conditions, our good fortune may not last
long. While enjoying a life of prosperity, people who
realize this truth will think of the many people who are
still living in poverty and are in need of assistance. Even
one compassionate thought of helping others can allow
us to plant a positive cause and reap the fruit of good fortune in the future. Otherwise, if we use up all our wealth
and lose our means to help, we will be unable to help the
poor even if we wanted to. Thus, we must practice kindness in a timely fashion.

4. Employing our influence can equip us to help our fellow
citizens. Some people may use the power and influence
they gain to either take advantage of others, especially
the kind and gentle, or to confer some benefit upon
humanity. Kindness or malice is only separated by a single thought hinging on our conscience and ability to realize the truth. Since "government is the ideal place to cultivate merits," people in high office should have some
consideration for their citizens. They should not use
their authority to take advantage of those they govern,
but resolve instead to find solutions to their problems and
difficulties.

In short, when we are always examining ourselves, we
will have less trouble in dealing with worldly matters. At the same
time, we can also benefit those around us even more.

Self-Improvement

"Learning is like rowing a boat upstream, we regress if we fail to make progress." In life, be it our studies, interactions with others, or the handling of problems, we all need to work constantly to improve. If we stick to our old ways and keep treading on the same spot, we will eventually find ourselves behind the times. Therefore, we must always strive to do better today than we did yesterday. With improvement, we will gain a sense of accomplishment, and find self-contentment. How do we improve? The following are some guidelines:

1. Refine our disposition by studying hard. If we want to progress, we first need to improve our disposition. We can do so by disciplining ourselves to apply our best effort. Many motivated scholars throughout Chinese history have set good examples by overcoming poverty and hardship, and working tirelessly day and night in their studies. However, learning or studying should not be limited to the pursuit of fame or fortune or the attainment of a good job. It should be to gain good reasoning, while improving our disposition as well. Scholars and literati of the past were never rude or vulgar. They were always genteel, well-poised, ethical, and righteous, possessing all the qualities associated with a refined disposition.

2. Renew ourselves by repenting. We need to abide by the laws and mores of society and safeguard our conduct with the rules of etiquette and morality. Trains are only safe when they run on their tracks, while cars are safe when drivers obey traffic rules. Likewise, if our conduct deviates from the right track, we must repent. Repentance is like Dharma water that can cleanse our

body and mind. If our clothes get dirty, washing them with soap and clear water will restore cleanliness. Therefore, we also need to know how to repent in order to keep renewing and improving ourselves.

3. Cultivate harmony with others. The most important aspect of self-improvement is to learn how to interact well with others and deal effectively with issues. If we are always fighting with others, marching to a different drum in everything we do, and bickering over small matters, people will find dealing with us a painful experience. We will not be able to enjoy positive connections with people but only end up being rejected by them. Therefore, in getting along with people, it is important to project an easy-going personality and cultivate harmony in human relationships. Together, these will offer us the greatest success in life.

4. Purify our mind with religious practice. Regardless of our faith, we must examine ourselves and practice on the right path. It is only through applying the right Way, that we can purify our body and mind in order to improve our character.

These guidelines are indispensable in seeking self-improvement.

Keys for Self-Discipline

We must have self-discipline in order to gain respect for ourselves and others. People who have self-discipline will naturally know how to manage their lives, so that their days are filled with peace and ease. Among those renowned for their longevity, Mr. Zhang Qun lived to the age of one hundred and one. He composed a "Self-Discipline Verse" which has become the motto for many people as the way to nurture life. The following are a few lines from his verse which can be used as guidelines for self-discipline:

1. Walk three thousand steps in the day, and sleep for seven hours at night. Walking is affirmed by athletes and medical professionals as an almost perfect form of exercise. Many people who visit their relatives in China discover that a lot of residents there live very long lives because they have the habit of walking everywhere they go. Buddhism teaches, "Walk a thousand steps on the Buddha's path, live life to the age of ninety-nine." The Buddhist scriptures also speak about the five benefits of walking: one can walk long distances, contemplate quietly, suffer less sickness, facilitate digestion, and maintain meditative concentration for long periods of time. We can thus walk our way towards good health.

   Sleep allows our body and mind to settle down into deep tranquility, so that we can recharge our energy and get rid of fatigue. However, if we are lazy and indulge in sleeping, we will become muddled without awareness. Therefore, most people only require seven to eight hours of sleep. When we sleep, we should learn to visualize brightness, and if we are adept in this practice, even our dreams will be full of light. When we cultivate sleeping in this way, our body and mind will benefit enormously.

2. Do not overeat, and keep a normal schedule for work and rest. Some kind of sustenance is necessary for all life. The *Discourse on the Classic of Buddha Land* states, "Sustaining the physical body so that it will not fall ill nurtures all benevolent dharmas." Indeed, food maintains our physical health, and when we eat properly, it also nurtures positive phenomena. Hence, the Buddha told King Prajnit, who was overweight, "People should be mindful of eating modestly so that they have a lighter load to carry. In turn, they would gain ease and comfort, along with the benefit of longevity." The Tang poet Bai Juyi also asserted, "A day has five periods; while work and rest each has its time." Truly capable people work and rest on a regular schedule. They appreciate the importance of balancing work and rest, because being overworked or unduly relaxed with a chaotic schedule will not help us with calm contemplation or problem solving. Thus, Buddhist practice emphasizes upholding a regular daily schedule that includes chanting and taking meals. It fully recognizes the importance of maintaining a proper time for work and for rest.

3. Embodying compassion within our mind, emitting fragrance with our words. The highest virtue in life is compassion. Compassionate people care for all sentient beings with a gentle heart, view all phenomena with eyes of loving-kindness, praise others with sincere words and joy, and conduct kind deeds with diligent effort. Compassionate conditions enrich life and enhance harmony. The sound of kind words is unforgettable and calms people like a gentle breeze. "With no anger, the mouth gives out wondrous fragrances." If we have no verbal blame or complaints, our mind is at peace. When we speak to others, there will be no sarcasm, harsh

words, lies, gossip, or slander. As the *Diamond Sutra* explains, all that is said will be "real words, truthful words, correct words, not false words and not changing words." When our words do not carry any knives or barbs, they will not hurt anyone. Only then will we "emit fragrance with our words."

4. Upholding the right Dharma with every thought, our aspiration for enlightenment will grow day by day. "Right thought" is having right thinking and views. In a meditation hall, the leading monastic often calls out, "Give rise to right thinking!" When taking a meditative meal, the monastic leading the chanting also calls out, "On hearing the sound of the bell, everyone upholds right thinking." They are reminding us to maintain right thoughts at all times in the day. Right thoughts can correct delusions and cure our worries. People with right thoughts are firm in their faith. They will keep fortifying themselves in conducting benevolent deeds, speaking kind words, and upholding positive thoughts. In practicing right action, right speech, and right thinking with our body, speech, and mind, we can benefit all sentient beings and enhance our aspiration for enlightenment.

The laws, rules, and regulations in the world are external restrictions imposed on us by others. On the other hand, the Buddhist precepts are demands we make of ourselves that come from within. They instill in us a self-discipline which allows us to place ourselves in the place of others, while being considerate of their needs. People with self-discipline do not trouble themselves or others, because they live life according to the right path.

Self-Discipline and Practicing Kindness

"Not giving rise to unwholesome thoughts is purifying ourselves; always practicing kindness is enriching society," asserts *Humble Table, Wise Fare.* Not giving rise to unwholesome thoughts is self-discipline, and practicing kindness is benefiting others. Self-discipline is working for our own merits; however, practicing kindness is the initiative we take to help and support all sentient beings and thus is beneficial to others. The following are some of the ways we can practice both:

1. Be upright and strict in self-discipline. Being upright and righteous should be the foundation of our conduct. People who examine themselves well are often very disciplined. While they are stern in dealing with their own faults, they are tolerant of the mistakes of others. They give others the chance to correct their errors, guiding them skillfully with wisdom and advice towards the right view. They exemplify "strict in self-discipline, tolerant in treating others."

2. Treat others with integrity and loyalty. In teaching others, it is better to be kind than strict; likewise, it is better to be tolerant than stern when dealing with others. If we treat others with a harsh attitude and deal with our own shortcomings with latitude and forgiveness, we lack integrity.

Loyalty, however, is the most precious quality in human relationships. Callous and treacherous people only terrify others while loyal and righteous ones win their trust and respect. Thus, we should not hesitate helping friends in need or give others financial assistance in emergencies, as such deeds can certainly bring warmth to the world.

3. Deal with matters with sincerity and diligence. Whether we are establishing a business, opening a factory, or working in a company, we must realize that no single matter can be completed by one person alone. It always takes a number of friends cooperating together or the joint effort of many people connected by various means to achieve success. Hence, we must rely on our sincerity and diligence to win over the recognition and trust of others in major undertakings. After all, sincerity is the foundation of success in our career and diligence its driving force. If all we do is expect others to take on hardships while we enjoy privileges, we cannot forge positive connections with people, and failure will not be far away.

4. Practice kindness with compassion and resolve. Buddhism teaches, "Phenomena do not arise by themselves; they rely on circumstances to become manifest." In this human world, self and others are connected as one. No one can live as an island because we must support one another in our accomplishments. Hence, we ought to help each other even in some small ways, because by doing so, we are actually helping ourselves. We should constantly practice benevolence and serve others with enthusiasm. People who consistently perform kind deeds usually have few unwholesome thoughts. As they abandon all unwholesomeness, they will gradually distance themselves from misfortune and create positive conditions for an improved fortune.

The *Gatha of the Seven Ancient Buddhas* warns, "Do not commit any unwholesomeness; uphold all benevolence." The former is based on self-discipline and the latter on the practice of kindness. Confucianism also espouses, "Look upon no impropriety; Listen to no impropriety; Speak no impropriety; Commit no impropriety." This too entails the practice of self-discipline. With self-discipline we can avert much trouble and build the foundation for personal cultivation and a successful career. The practice of kindness curbs greed and desire, which in turn is the best prescription for harmonious human relationships. Together, self-discipline and benevolence can bring all of us endless good fortune and a long life.

Self-Development

We often see people opening factories, creating new products, developing new land or exploring new energy resources and minerals. While some of us might develop new external resources, we do not have to go outside of ourselves for development, because we all have endless treasures within ourselves. How to develop ourselves is truly the most important lesson in life. The following are some guidelines for self-development:

1. Look for flavor in simplicity. Are you finding life too simple? We get up in the morning and go to bed at night, eat three meals a day, and go to work everyday. Life may indeed seem quite plain. However, we can look for flavor in the routine of life – the taste of simplicity. What is the taste of simplicity? For instance, we can be happy, safe, peaceful, free, unoccupied, and relaxed. When we can experience all of these in our daily life, a simple life actually can have many flavors.

2. Look for contentment in labor. We all have to work hard every day. If we consider work a hardship, then naturally it will be difficult. If we find joy, interest, and a sense of achievement in our work, then it will become our source of happiness. If we enjoy working because of the joy it gives us, we will live experience happiness everyday.

3. Look for freedom in confinement. Do we find our world, living quarters, or social circle too small? Do we feel confined within ourselves? Yet within a restricted lifestyle, our mind can still be free and liberated. We can

broaden our thinking and enhance our resolve. Moreover, we can embrace the entire Dharma realm within our mind. As long as we can cultivate the world of our body and mind, we will be able to find our niche.

4. Look for true love in friendships. According to the saying, "Between nobility and lowliness, it is easy to tell the depth of one's friendship." The flux in human relationships and worldly matters can truly be heart-rending. While sentiments and affection between people can run really thin, there can be hope for us if we take the initiative to change. If we find people around us cold and indifferent, we should not be frustrated. We should warm up to others instead with sincerity and devotion, then naturally, we can find true love in our friendships.

These four guidelines are essential for self-development.

Self-Strengthening

We start our life being taught by our parents at home. Parents put in all that effort with the hope that their sons or daughters will succeed to become models of accomplishment. In school, teachers too provide us with the morals and knowledge to be wise and noble. As we enter the workforce, coworkers and supervisors give us advice and support us with the hope that we can make steady progress. However, it is insufficient if we always rely on others to educate and help us. We must strengthen ourselves, and the following are some keys for doing so:

1. Self-knowledge helps us to understand propriety. It is important for us to know ourselves. Otherwise, the consequences will give us trouble. If we do not know ourselves, we will not see the big picture. We would have no idea of circumstances, causes, and conditions. Moreover, we would not know what others need nor appreciate propriety, nor would we know where we are heading or where we came from. It is neither healthy nor complete.

2. Self-respect helps us to resist temptation. "People must have self-respect before others respect them." By the same token, "People must insult themselves before they are insulted by others." If we are scorned or looked down upon, it is often the result of our own lack of self-respect. According to the saying, "The virtuous will not be honored if they lack self-respect." If we do not have self-respect or lack self-control, it will be easy for us to succumb to external temptation and naturally attract unnecessary insults. Therefore, it is imperative to have self-respect.

3. Self-reliance helps us to survive independently.
   According to the saying, "you can rely on a mountain,
   but it can collapse; you can rely on people, but they will
   get old." Though all things arise from the right combi-
   nation of conditions, we need to bear in mind that they
   are only supporting ones. We cannot depend solely upon
   them because worldly matters are impermanent and
   always subject to change. We need to also rely on ourselves. When we are able to establish ourselves independently, we can be our own master and gain strength.
   We can take the initiative in doing whatever we want to
   do. If we cannot even establish ourselves, how then can
   we help others to do the same?

4. Self-confidence helps us to live in ease and peace.
   "There are endless treasures within the gates of confidence." Faith and confidence are indeed our supreme
   treasures. We need to have faith in ourselves. For this
   reason, Buddhism places much emphasis on establishing
   the "Four Incorruptible Faiths," which include faith in
   the Triple Gem, the Four Noble Truths, the Way of the
   teacher, and our true Buddha nature. If we can establish
   self-confidence, then there is nothing too difficult in the
   world for us to accomplish. We can go anywhere and be
   able to get help from all sides. Hence, with self-confidence, we will certainly live in peace and ease.

We must therefore strengthen ourselves and not just rely on others. When we know how to educate ourselves, we will be able to
strengthen and establish ourselves.

Four Keys to Self-Discipline

People tend to make demands on others as to what to say or do. If their demands are not met, they get angry easily and may even turn friends into enemies. Actually, it is more important to make demands on ourselves rather than on others. People with self-discipline have dignity and can win the respect of others. The following are four keys to self-discipline:

1. Have our own views so we will not easily succumb to what others say. Some people have no opinion themselves and easily follow what others say regardless of right or wrong. They are unsure of their own viewpoint, bending every which way the wind blows like weeds on top of a wall. Having no views of their own, they simply repeat what others claim. Instead of always listening, having nothing to offer on any issue, and not being our own master, we need to have our own position and viewpoint so that we will not easily succumb to what others say. No one should be led by the nose on every matter.

2. Live independently so we do not have to lean on others. When baby birds mature, they fly away from their nests. Similarly, animals leave their mothers when they are fully grown to live on their own. We cannot keep leaning on others, asking our parents for money, looking for our relatives' support or hoping for society to provide us with endless resources. We need to live independent lives. In addition to self-sufficiency and strengthening ourselves, we should also help others when we have the means to do so.

3. Be open and frank so we do not covertly criticize others.

It is said in the *Book of Rites*, "Scrutinized by ten pairs of eyes and singled out by ten pair of hands, how can we not be self-disciplined?" Lu Qiuyuan, a renowned philosopher of the Song Dynasty, asserted, "The ancients were cautious with what they should not see or hear, so that they would not engage in frivolous gossip." People who are open and frank in whatever they say and do also conduct themselves righteously everywhere they go. They will not discuss the strengths or shortcomings of others, step on them when they are down, or quibble with them over gains or losses. If we fail to uphold ethics in our speech and instead dwell on criticizing others, we must realize that other people will also do the same to us. Moreover, when what is said behind people's back finds its way to their ears, it not only hurts and disappoints the victims, but it will also come back to haunt us.

4. Be righteous and just so we will not harm others. A Yuan Dynasty scholar once said, "One who acts righteously is a true gentleman of integrity and selflessness." Righteous people have no ulterior motives and will not scheme in the dark to harm another. Even if they are alone by themselves, they will still uphold morals and do nothing shameful. As the saying goes, "The gentleman does not take advantage of a dark room."

The Song Dynasty scholar Lin Pu's "Reflections of the Mind," points out: "Money can gather people, self-discipline can overcome people, magnanimity can win over people, and initiative can lead people." Self-knowledge and self-discipline are keys for establishing ourselves and dealing with the world. Tolerating and supporting others are keys for harmony in human relationships. People who are good at critiquing others are poor at observing themselves. On the other hand, those who can examine themselves well are surely self-disciplined.

Be a Complete People

According to the saying, "People who can endure the worst suffering are supreme." However, in conducting ourselves, we do not necessarily have to be supreme. It is more important to be wise, righteous, kind, and good, the qualities of a complete person. How do we become a complete person? The following are some guidelines:

1. Do not be a foolish person; be wise. People are sometimes deluded and unreasonable. Therefore, when they are working with others, they can cause much trouble and worry to both themselves and others. The biggest problem with foolish people is their attachment to self. They just cannot listen to the advice of others. As a result, no matter how rational the advice is, it is still beyond their understanding. It is very difficult getting along with people like that. Hence, some people say, "I'd rather argue with an intelligent person than speak to a foolish one." Indeed, we must be wise and not foolish.

2. Do not be a deviant person; be righteous. "When a righteous person gives a distorted teaching, it will become right; when a perverted person give a correct teaching, it will become distorted." Whatever a perverted person speaks or does and the ideas they propagate can often bring irreparable harm to society that will linger for a long time. Therefore, we must strive to be a righteous person who can benefit society and not a perverted one whom everyone rejects.

3. Do not be a malicious person; be kind. Kind and mali-

cious thoughts within our mind arise and cease endlessly everyday. Therefore, the gap between being kind or malicious often lies within one thought. Buddhism regards people who indulge in killing, stealing, sexual misconduct, telling lies, taking drugs as malicious. In addition, they are regarded as divisive, harsh, and irrational in speech, and full of greed, anger and ignorance. They will sooner or later be rejected by others everywhere they go. Ultimately then, we must transform all unwholesome deeds into benevolent ones in order to become a kind person.

4. Do not be inhuman; be complete. What is a complete person? Someone with morals and ethics is a complete person. In the Buddhist scriptures, the Buddha once taught his disciples not to exhibit the five kinds of "inhumanity." The meaning of "inhumanity" is someone who has the form of a human in terms of having eyes, ears, nose, mouth, and a body, but his or her behavior, thinking, and character do not belong to that of a being human. For instance, people like that have no appreciation for kindness, show no joy when they should be joyous, and do not laugh when they should. As such, they do not act like a human being. We cannot be inhuman, because we must be a complete person.

It is impossible for people to be perfect. However, we can be a complete person if we are patient and willing to accept disadvantages for the sake of the common good. We should think positively about every matter and be considerate of others in all situations in life. When we learn to be a kind person with wisdom and righteousness, we will certainly succeed in life.

useful People

We all want to be useful in life. Even with less than favorable causes and conditions, a useful person can have "hands of gold" that produce resounding success. On the other hand, if a major project is undertaken by someone who is inept, it will turn out badly. How do we become a useful person? The following points offer some advice:

1. We must be like the pine and cypress withstanding the elements. Life is not always smooth sailing and we cannot always get what we want. People who are truly useful can overcome their setbacks, and thus distinguish themselves from others in their capacity and capabilities. They are able to overcome obstacles, accept disadvantages, and bear hardships. We have to tolerate the injustice of human sentiments and suffer the wrongs of worldly matters before we can transcend and rise to a higher level. Only then can we be compared to the thousand-year-old pines and cypresses.

2. We must be like sense organs fulfill their functions. Buddhism calls the human eyes, ears, nose, tongue, body, and mind the "six roots." The eyes see, the ears hear, the nose smells, and the tongue tastes as they all fulfill in their respective functions. If a person can function appropriately in any circumstance and relationship, like Avalokitesvara Bodhisattva manifesting in myriads of forms depending on the need, then he or she can be considered a useful person.

3. The point is not for us to be omnipotent; we just need the

will to try. It is like a blind person and a crippled one cooperating with each other: the blind can carry the crippled and the latter can provide directions for the both of them. Working well together, they can get out of a difficult situation. Therefore, we should never insist on our own views nor try to do everything by ourselves. We need to realize that people rely on many causes and conditions for survival. When we know how to support each other, we become useful people.

4. We must be like the wise and virtuous not belittling beginners. "Seek the Dharma through respect." Respect is not just what subordinates show their superiors. "Not belittling beginners" is also a form of respect people should have. A capable person may be a wise and virtuous person already. However, if one shows respect for subordinates, they will gain due respect in return. Therefore, the truly wise and virtuous do not just focus on how much they can achieve. They are happy to provide others with positive causes and conditions, and space to develop. Having the magnanimity to give newcomers a helping hand is the true sign of a wise and virtuous person.

Judging whether or not a person is useful depends on how much of their capacity and ability can be demonstrated. Truly useful people should be able to either rise to the occasion or be content in a minor position. They can stand on the front lines or remain in the background. Furthermore, they need to be able to withstand hot and cold or hunger and deprivation. They must be either vocal or quiet depending on the situation, and satisfied with either having or not having responsibilities.

Conditions for Being Useful

Most people want to be useful. With the exception of those who indulge in immorality or self-indulgence, no one likes to be useless. However, whether we are useful or not depends on our willingness to be giving. Some people may be skillful in a certain field, but they refuse to serve others. They do not want to contribute their expertise to society. In the end, they are not useful even though they may have the ability to do so.

On the contrary, there are people who have no special skills, but they are very hard working and willing to serve others. Consequently, everyone likes them and considers them indispensable. Thus, they will always be assigned a supporting role to play even if they have no special skills. What then are the key conditions for being useful? The following are some suggestions:

1. High morals: Ethics are fundamental to being human. We may not be intelligent or skillful, but we cannot be without morals. Buddhism teaches compassion, joy, generosity, humility, and gratitude. These are the essentials in conducting ourselves. Confucianism advocates the "three bonds and five virtues" and the "four ethical principles and eight cardinal virtues" which are ethics we all should have. Today's society emphasizes punctuality, trustworthiness, service, and charity. Moreover, not smoking or drinking nor taking drugs are also wholesome practices, representing the basic conduct for human beings. If we are only learned and talented but lacking in morals, we will most likely become the victims of our own gifts. Thus in order to make ourselves truly useful, we must first elevate our morals.

2. Wealth in knowledge: If we want to establish a success-

ful career, being knowledgeable is a prerequisite. It is fine to be an expert in a certain field, but in the complex world of today, we also need a general understanding of other subjects. We should first be broad in our learning and then proceed to go deeper into a special field in order to fully realize our talents. In short, if we want to establish ourselves in society, we need to be broad in learning, exposing ourselves to all kinds of knowledge. We should equip ourselves with the worldly knowledge of the citizen, the spiritual cultivation of a practitioner, the practical expertise of a volunteer, and even the transcendental awareness of existence itself.

3. A kind and gentle personality: a person's character is a decisive factor for his or her achievements. There are capable and talented people who are loners. They do not fit well into any group or organization, because they are reclusive, arrogant, and selfish. As such, their achievements will naturally be limited. If we want to be truly useful, we must be willing to help others and follow conditions accordingly. We need to be considerate, forgiving, and tolerant. In addition, we should always be ready to offer our service and allow others space to maneuver so that they will enjoy working with us. In doing so, we will gain a good reputation and the support of others.

4. Good health: There is an old saying, "As long as the mountain stays green, there will always be firewood for the future." Our health is fundamental to all achievements. If we are not in good health, it will be difficult for us to realize any ideal. Therefore, besides having a wealth of knowledge, high morals, and a kind personality, we also need good health before we can bring our talents into full play and become a truly useful person.

Hence, taking care of our health regularly is a key factor
for success.

It is better for one to be useless than to be unreasonable.
Ideally, it is best if we can all be useful and reasonable at the same
time. If we want to be a useful person, we should be mindful of
the above.

Upholding Ourselves

Management science has gained much popularity these days, and people are interested in how to better manage everything from a corporation, finances, filing systems, human resources, and even to our emotions. In fact, it is most important to manage ourselves well. How can we best manage who we are? The following are some keys for doing so:

1. Do not take credit ahead of others. Whether we run our own business or work in a company, we should not contend for honor and profit. We should be more generous in spirit, sharing whatever gains we have with others, so that we can benefit them and protect ourselves at the same time. According to an ancient classic, "Ministers do not base their success on profit and honor." During the Qing Dynasty, a renowned general was bestowed the top honor by the Emperor Yongzheng after some major victories. However, the general grew to be so arrogant that even the emperor became suspicious. In the end, as others in the imperial court joined together to sabotage the general, he was sent to jail where he eventually died. This account illustrates the negative consequences of taking credit ahead of others. *Humble Table, Wise Fare* reminds us, "Where there is no way to advance, we should know how to retreat; where there is a way to progress, we should know how to yield credit to others."

2. Do not fall behind others in morals. "Establishing a good name is not as good as cultivating morals." Because of the differences in our abilities and intelligence, our personal wealth, career, knowledge, and reputation vary in many ways. However, we should not allow external cir-

cumstances to compromise our morals, compassion, character, humility, and ethical cultivation. While we may often lag behind others in terms of worldly achievements, we should not fall behind in terms of ethical cultivation. We can be without money or worldly possessions, but we should never be lacking in morals. "A precious word of truth is worth much more than any amount of gold and silver; valuable ethics and morals are infinitely taller than any hill or mountain. Hence, we should always be more compassionate, have higher morals, and show greater humility. With consistent effort, our virtues will pervade over time.

3. Do not be indulgent in pleasures. There are so many things to enjoy in life, such as good food, nice clothes, a comfortable home, or travel to different places. Furthermore, we enjoy being praised, loved, protected and cared for. Regardless of how much enjoyment is available, the key is not to be indulgent nor take what we do not deserve, because excesses in any matter will not be beneficial. For instance, we should reflect on the extent of our contribution to work to see if it is commensurate with the salary we receive each month. We should only take what we truly deserve. It is actually not in our best interest if we obtain what is beyond our worth. Accordingly, we should "not try to claim too much honor with just a little knowledge and virtue." We should not belittle our contributions in life nor should we inflate them by enjoying undue privileges.

4. Do not digress from the middle path in speech and actions. "One's capabilities can be seen from one's actions; one's moral cultivation can be detected from one's speech." A useful phrase is superior to a thousand

useless words; a single beneficial deed is better than useless hard work. However, most people are too extreme
in conducting themselves, dealing with matters, or
speaking to others. When they are happy, what they say
lacks propriety, and when they get angry, their conduct is
often abrasive. They are either too strict or lenient in
making demands on others. It is best if we can keep to
the middle path in our speech and actions by being neither temperamental nor indifferent, and by neither seeking nor rejecting others.

There are certainly standards for interpersonal relations,
such as knowing when to advance and retreat, and maintaining self-
respect and dignity. The above four ways for upholding ourselves
provide us with guidelines for proper conduct.

Sculpturing Ourselves

"Without polishing, jade cannot become an ornament; without learning, people will not appreciate morals" according to *The Three-Character Classic*. People are like jade and precious gems: we need to constantly polish ourselves by learning from one another through the exchange of views. We must keep molding ourselves so that we can be well-rounded and mature. The following are some guidelines on how to sculpture ourselves:

1. Develop our wisdom. Wisdom is not just something spoken or written in books. True wisdom comes from within our mind. In Buddhism, developing the wisdom of our mind-field is called "understanding one's mind and seeing one's nature." Once the wisdom of our mind-field is developed with the manifestation of the "great perfect mirror wisdom," we will be able to appreciate all phenomena of the universe in all their various forms and colors. Wisdom differs from worldly intelligence and cleverness. Therefore, wisdom is not sought from without but only from within our mind. Once we have prajna-wisdom, we can better understand the truth.

2. Be gentle in temperament. Some people have a hot temper and may insist they were born that way. There are also lazy people who self-righteously declare laziness is their birthright. Others may be greedy or enjoy fighting. However, our personality should never be violent or temperamental. We should not indulge in mood swings doing whatever pleases us. We need to modify our disposition through molding ourselves and correcting our faults, so that we can be in harmony with the rest of society and be accepted by others.

3. Be optimistic in dealing with challenges. It is inevitable that we will come across people we do not like. Some people lose faith from the slightest conflict, either considering their friends unworthy or their efforts unnecessary. In reality, life is filled with disappointments, so we need to maintain optimism in our heart and be less demanding of others. Often, we too quickly reject others for their inadequacies, but if we have a little more compassion and help them instead, everything will change for the better. Hence, a life faced with optimism will be much more beautiful.

4. Strengthen our morality. In getting along with people, we need morals and ethics to sustain us. The higher our morals, the nobler our character. When morality is the foundation for all our exchange with others, our virtues will naturally be noble and pure. Therefore, in molding ourselves, we especially need to improve our conduct and strengthen our morals. We should not be making demands on other people, because it is always better to demand more of ourselves.

In order to establish ourselves in society, besides good health, it is imperative that we polish our wisdom, disposition, thinking, and ethics, diligently strengthening ourselves so that we can bring our abilities and capacity into full play.

Improving Ourselves

We all have some undesirable tendencies and habits that must be corrected from time to time. We also have unwholesome views and conduct that need to be improved. People who know how to improve will progress in life. However, those who cling to their old ways and righteously declare, "That's the way I am" will never be able to progress. The following are some guidelines on how to improve ourselves:

1. It is better to be active than passive. Some people are generally passive, lacking spirit and energy. They always appear lazy and have no courage to take on any challenge. People with a passive disposition must change for the better, because nothing can be gained by living a passive life. Passivity needs to be transformed into activeness so we can move forward in life. Only then will we be able to carve out our own world. In whatever we do, we have to actualize it one step at a time, in order to succeed and share the results.

2. It is better to take initiative than to act on orders. Some people are like pawns in a chess game. They only make a step when someone moves them. They will do nothing unless others ask them to work. It is impossible for such people to achieve any accomplishment. Therefore, we must take the initiative in volunteering our service, working hard at our job, or acting benevolently towards others. The world is controlled by those who take the initiative. Only people who are actively involved can truly become a valuable part of a team, thereby expanding their life.

3. It is better to optimistic than pessimistic. Besides being passive, some people are also pessimistic. They look at their future, career, and family with pessimism. They do not have hope for their friends, country, and society. The following tale offers a moral on finding happiness:

A puppy kept chasing his tail all the time, spinning around in circles because someone had told him his tail is where happiness is. However, he could never catch his tail. An older dog later advised him, "Happiness is actually in front of us. When you keep moving ahead, happiness will follow you." The moral of this story reminds pessimistic people that if they think differently, then the world will no longer be filled with clouds of sorrow. When we can transform sadness into joy, be active, optimistic, and have self-confidence, then happiness will surely surround us.

4. It is better to be supple than rigid. "A steel blade is likely to injure someone; a rigid bow breaks its string easily." There are people with bad temper who stare at others with angry eyes, curse or use abusive language, or even punch people with their fists over trivial matters. They are hurtful and create enemies everywhere they go, and they are the ones who end up being hurt most of all. In the long run, suppleness overcomes rigidity. Thus, we should treat others with tolerance and kindness, so our presence will be like a gentle spring breeze. In time, we will be able to meet with positive opportunities anywhere we go, and gain success in everything we do. Gentleness and tolerance are the best prescriptions for dealing with people and matters.

The best education in life is based on self-awareness and self-enlightenment. People who know how to improve themselves will inevitably progress and mature.

Fortifying Ourselves

"Just as heaven follows its course persistently, the virtuous strengthen themselves incessantly." The greatest power begins with one's self-confidence. We must master it before we can further strengthen and establish ourselves. We all seek happiness in life, but it is not bestowed by heaven or given to us by another person. Happiness and joy can only be gained by our self-reliance and endless impulse to create. The following are some keys on how to fortify ourselves:

1. Let go of the shame from previous failures. Some people fail once and cannot accept such a setback, so they become mired in a sinking or hopeless feeling. In reality, if we can learn from experience, every failure and set-back can be the impetus to move us forward. The tougher the defeat, the stronger the drive to progress. Every mistake is in fact a lesson. As long as we do not give up in the face of setbacks, we will be able to cultivate our strength on a deeper lever. Therefore, if we fall down, we must stand up again with courage, so we can go much farther.

2. Get rid of improper conduct. We need to constantly review our actions, speech, and thinking, especially in how we carry ourselves. We must conduct ourselves according to morals. If we break the law, act illicitly or unethically, or go against the norms of the community, we must change for the better. If we do not correct our errant behavior, it will only end up a burden that will obstruct our future.

3. Wipe away selfish thoughts. The gravest ill in life is selfishness. A narrow-minded person will bicker and contend with others on every matter, thus making it impossible to achieve any major accomplishment in life. Yet, it is indeed very difficult for most people, who are by nature selfish, to refrain from working for their own benefit. This selfish thinking can drive them to create their own negative karma through committing unwholesome deeds. Hence, we must do our best to eradicate selfish thoughts from our mind. When we can be selfless and just, our mind will be open and bright, allowing us to live in peace and harmony with others.

4. Forget the embarrassment of insults. In the course of life, even the greatest person will inevitably be insulted and feel hurt. For instance, Jesus was betrayed by his disciple and crucified on the cross. Sakyamuni Buddha was slandered by Devadatta and even physically injured. In Chinese history, the renowned general Han Xin was made to crawl under another man's legs, while Su Qin had to bear the humiliation of his own parents disowning him. The more embarrassing the insults, the more we should leave them behind in order to gain strength for progress.

"Becoming generals or ministers is not predestined; the true gentleman strengthens himself." In life, we should all strive to fortify ourselves to gain self-confidence.

Perfecting Ourselves

We need to be demanding of ourselves and seek to be complete as individuals. We should not wait for others to ask us to improve. If we are not up to standard, then naturally there will be some who will be critical of us, pointing out our shortcomings and weaknesses. Yet if we make demands of ourselves in how we speak, handle situations and matters, or even in how we walk and sit, other people will have no reason to criticize. In fact, they will want us on their side. The following are some guidelines on perfecting ourselves:

1. Morality can win over others. *Humble Table, Wise Fare* teaches "Subduing others with power is only temporary and ineffective; moving others with ethics lasts over time and is highly effective." Regardless of how powerful one is, he or she can only subdue others temporarily and cannot truly win people's hearts. However, if we conduct ourselves with integrity and righteousness, speak to others with compassion, treat others with tolerance, and engage in social services with enthusiasm, people will have high regard for our morality and be willing to follow us.

2. Magnanimity can encompass others. If we want to pursue major undertakings, we first need the necessary skills and equally important, magnanimity. We must be tolerant of others. For instance, if they make mistakes, we have to forgive them. We must be forgiving of their weaknesses, allowing them time and room to learn and grow. We should never be harsh on others yet easy on our own faults. One must apply "the inclination to blame others to oneself, and the instinct to forgive oneself to

others," before one can truly embrace others. People who are filled with loving-kindness will naturally attract others from near and far. In this way, they will have no fear of failure.

3. Integrity can convince others. First impressions are very important when meeting people. However, we should never assess a person's character based on first impressions. "It takes time to know a person's heart" according to a popular saying. Therefore, through our relationships, people will discover our true character over time, be it our loyalty and nobleness, or our hypocrisy and treachery. It is only by being sincere and trustworthy that friendships can be made to last.

4. We can move others when feelings are sincere. True love and true feelings work best in moving people. In history, kings and emperors were able to win the undying loyalty of their ministers and generals because of the depth of their feelings for them. Many old servants who were treated as part of the family by their employers would serve their benefactors for a lifetime. Because both were moved by the depth of mutual feelings, they were able to sustain a life-long relationship. In treating people, our genuine feelings can certainly gain their respect and loyalty towards us.

Therefore, we must first try to perfect ourselves before others will be willing to follow us. Through our experience with people and matters, we can slowly improve ourselves.

Living in the World

Born into this world, we cannot distance ourselves from daily life even when practicing a religion. Hence, the practice of Chan masters in the past never departed from the basic necessities of "go eat," "have tea," "eat when hungry, sleep when tired" or even the "need to take a pee." In the course of a day, how can any one of us detach ourselves from the mundane world? Whether we are followers of a religion or not, we all need to live a worldly life. The following are some guidelines to consider:

1. We need to embody the worldly spirit to progress. The most common criticism leveled at religions is that they encourage followers to be too passive and detached. Some practitioners in turn believe that the spirit of cultivation lies in extreme asceticism and solipsism. In fact, it is people with religious faith who need to exhibit the strength of action and initiative to better the world. Chan Master Huangbo once exhorted "Cut off your two legs" to dismiss the narrow spirit of mere self-liberation. Chan Master Daoyuan's retort "If you don't sun them [mushrooms] now, then when?" advocates a similar sense of urgency. Both illustrate the expediency of making the best use of the here and now. Hence, true cultivation is not having too many fears or hesitation about the next step; instead, we need to realize fully the Mahayana spirit of sacrifice and contribution aimed at benefiting self and others.

2. We need to speak the truth with optimism and joy. When discussing their faith, religious followers need not constantly speak about "seeing beyond the world," "carrying the enmity and debt from previous lives," "waiting to be

born into heaven," or "rebirth in the Pure Land," nor should they talk incessantly about "impermanence," "suffering," or "emptiness." They are merely quoting from a text and not correctly understanding the Law of Dependent Origination. People who truly appreciate the truth of religion speak to inspire confidence and hope, sharing their Dharma joy and peace of mind with people around them. In this way, they are speaking the truth with optimism and joy.

3. We need to have self-supporting enterprises that benefit the public. As religious leaders, we cannot rely on the support and assistance of others all the time. While devotees make donations to provide us with food and clothing, we still need to have our enterprises to support ourselves and also benefit the public. Monastics can till the land, plant trees, protect the environment, build roads and bridges, train people, and teach and help all sentient beings with the Dharma. There are so many areas in which we can become involved in order to create revenue and benefit humanity. When we work to fulfill the needs of all sentient beings, we are contributing positively to the human world.

4. We need the elements of compassion, wisdom, vows, and practice. In Chinese Mahayana Buddhism, Avalokitesvara Bodhisattva of Mount Putuo in Nanhai represents great compassion, Manjusri Bodhisattva of Mount Wutai in Shanxi is the symbol of great wisdom, Ksitigarbha Bodhisattva of Mount Qiuhua in Anhui is the realization of great vow, and Samantabhadra Bodhisattva of Mount Emei in Sichuan is the exemplar of great practice. Therefore, as religious practitioners, we should learn from the characters of these great beings in order to fully

apply our faith in the world. "Buddhahood is attained when the human character is perfected." When our responsibilities and cultivation in the human world are completed, we can be assured of attaining Buddhahood.

Everyone in the world hopes for freedom from worry and fear in the present and future. Extreme practitioners may want to "go to hot places to endure the heat, and cold places to withstand the chill." Moderate practitioners on the other hand may want to live amongst "high mountains and meandering rivers with green willows and red flowers, or places that are warm when the sun shines and cool when the wind blows." We should be able to live anywhere if we can follow these guidelines for worldly living, and still reach the state of truth, benevolence, and beauty.

How to Face the World

In dealing with the world, we cannot depart from people. So if we want smooth sailing in life, we first need to understand human nature. Once we know how to deal with people, it will be easy to face the world. The following are four keys in facing the world:

1. Ridiculing others is the main cause for trouble. People with ethics will not ridicule what others say or do. According to the *Sutra of Forty-two Sections*, "When one uses harsh words on others, it is like giving someone an unwelcome present. If the other person refuses it, one needs to take it back." Telling lies and using harsh words are "like spitting toward the heavens: the spit will not reach heaven but will fall back onto one's face." Taunting others is "like shaking dust against the wind: the dust will not be blown away but will land on one's body." Therefore, in ridiculing others with our speech, we are asking for trouble. It is a tendency we must guard against.

2. Tolerating others is the key to gain good fortune. If we treat others with magnanimity instead of quarreling over minor faults, we will gain their support. We will distance ourselves from trouble by not transgressing on others. If we have no trouble in life, we are already blessed with good fortune. Therefore, tolerating others is the key to a blessed life. We all seek good fortune in life, but it does not come from being calculating and bickering with others over small matters. Moreover, even if we are blamed or wronged, we should not bear any grudges or fight with others; and in time, good fortune will come.

3. Subjugating others with power incurs hatred. People in high places with power often tend to subdue and strike others down with their authority. Do not think that this is victory for them because their actions are only instilling hatred that will haunt them in the future. Once they lose power, others will find the opportunity to get even. Therefore, in dominating others with power, we will face trouble in the future.

4. Treating others ethically ensures a good reputation. Regardless of whom we are dealing with, morals should be the foundation of our behavior and speech. For instance, in a business partnership or working jointly with others in any endeavor, we must make morals the top priority. Thus, we will distance ourselves from any transgressions and be able to gain a good reputation over time.

This is how we should be more vigilant of these four keys in facing the world.

The Way to Success

Life is like running a marathon. If we want to succeed, we must persevere till the end. As *Humble Table, Wise Fare* explains, "Self-learning is the force behind success, self-discipline is the condition for success, self-confidence is the method for success, and self-respect is the key for success." Success is not really difficult as long as we have these various qualifications, causes, and conditions. The following are some further guidelines for success:

1. We can be assured of a place in society when we have special skills. According to the saying, "Being in possession of great financial wealth is not as good as having a special skill." In order to establish ourselves in today's society, we must have special skills and knowledge. For instance, we need to be competent in either computers, accounting, making plans, writing, or driving. Modern society focuses on professionalism and specialization, so it will be difficult for us to find our place if we do not possess some expertise or special knowledge. Therefore, in order to survive in the world and make a living, it is imperative for us to learn several specialized skills.

2. We can be assured of forging ahead when we have hope. People survive on hope because with hope there is a future; and with hope, we will be able to realize our goals. Hikers, toiling and sweating, climb over ridges and mountains. They have no fear of hardship because in their hearts is the hope of reaching the summit. On our journey of life, the path may be long and rugged, and yet with hope, we are not afraid no matter how long the road may be. Hence, when we have hope we can bravely

forge ahead in whatever we do.

3. We can be assured of steady progress when we have diligence. We all want a better tomorrow and a brighter future. In order to do so, we must keep improving without slacking off. The ancients asserted, "Diligence can make up for slowness." In everything we do, as long as we work hard in applying ourselves, we will make steady progress, be it great or small. A never-ceasing trickle of water can cut through rock, and the constant friction of twigs can start a fire. When we are always diligent in what we do, we can keep improving and success will be ours.

4. We can be assured of prime opportunities when we have foresight. Handling worldly matters is like playing a game of chess. It is people with foresight who will win. Farsighted people are more likely to embrace good opportunities early on and achieve success. On the contrary, people who just pay attention to what is close at hand are shallow in their views. They can only see themselves and not the general public; they can only see their families and not the entire community; they can only see the small profits in front of their eyes but not the broad picture into the future. People like that confine themselves to small frames and are naturally limited in what they can achieve.

We all admire success, but it does not fall from the sky for there must be proper causes and conditions. There is a way to success, so we should be mindful of these guidelines.

Thinking to Achieve

It is wonderful if people are well endowed. However, like Zeng Shen, the disciple of Confucius, was slow in learning, but he kept driving himself with "others may just do it once, I will do it ten times." In addition, he reflected on his mistakes daily and was honored as the "saint of the school" in the end. From this we can appreciate when there is diligence, perseverance, and ambition, we can certainly progress toward a life of goodness. Our worst fear is that we cannot apply ourselves in what we do and end up perishing like dead grass and shrubs. Therefore, every object and matter in the world, including the philosophies of life, are all contained in how we think. When we have right thinking, we will be able to move on to a benevolent life. The following is a short summary on this point:

1. If water does not move, the river becomes muddy. According to the *Spring and Autumn Annals*, "Flowing water remains fresh." If water does not flow, it turns into a smelly cesspool because it must keep moving in order to remain clean. It is the same with money. Money must be used in order for its value to truly function, otherwise gold bars stored under the bed are no different from pieces of stone. By the same token, we humans need to renew our thinking and knowledge all the time. Our lifestyle must keep changing, and our relationships will remain connected by frequent exchanges. As a result, we can keep in step with the changing times so that we do not fall behind.

2. If our resolve is not strong, we cannot reach our ideals. Many people have resolutions at a young age. We may want to grow up to become an engineer, an astronaut, a

teacher, or a doctor. However, over the years, we easily forget the resolutions we have made. Scholar Wang Yangming asserted, "Those who are not diligent in learning have a weak resolve." People who have a strong will and ambition will keep overcoming difficulties and breaking through obstacles in their effort to realize their goals. On the other hand, people whose resolve is not firm will easily be distracted by external matters. They will not be able to accomplish anything with what they have learned.

3. If our words lack trust, our actions cannot come to fruition. Confucius said, "If a person has no credibility, no one knows what they will do!" If what we say is not believable and we fail to keep our promise, our actions will not gain the approval of others, and we cannot gain any positive results either with what we do. Once our credibility fails, then no matter what we say later on, others will not believe in us anymore, and none of our suggestions will be accepted. Therefore, "a promise is worth a thousand pieces of gold," "once something is said, even four swift horses cannot retrieve it." Therefore, in conducting ourselves, we must have credibility in what we say.

4. If we do not think, we cannot achieve. People are thinking beings. If we do not want to use our brain and are reluctant to explore the reasoning of matters, we will fail to accomplish anything in our studies or career. Buddhism teaches, "Enter into meditative concentration through hearing, thinking, and practicing." Moreover, "Major enlightenment comes from major doubt; small enlightenment comes from small doubt; no enlightenment comes from no doubt." Therefore, whether we

want to achieve something in our studies, our career, or in our cultivation, we must think well in every matter. By being able to contemplate deeply, we can appreciate the core of the problem, and thereby find a way to improve and make further progress.

An important factor in deciding our success is whether our thinking is right or not. Life is an endless lesson, so we should not say "no" so easily. In our actions and thoughts, we should never have negative thinking and behaviors. Therefore, it is worth our while to contemplate deeply on thinking about how we can make our achievements.

Setting Our Own Traps

As we work and establish ourselves in society, people sometimes set traps so that we might fall into them. However, there are times when we set our own traps without even realizing it, leaving no way to free ourselves. This is indeed sad and most regrettable. What are the traps we set for ourselves? The following are some clues:

1. Worrying narrows our world. Some people live in anxiety and depression, unable to see through their plight. If we are unable to transcend our worries, then even though the world is open and wide, our own domain will be closed and narrow. It is like what happens to the open sky once dark clouds begin to gather, for even the sun or moon will lose its brightness. Therefore, we need to walk out of the shadow of our worries and open up our heart, so that our world will become open and wide once more.

2. Blaming provokes enmity. Some people tend to create animosity with others because they fail to think of the positive side of things. When speaking to others, they caw like crows; when dealing with people, they battle with them like fighting cocks. As they fight with everyone, they make enemies everywhere they go. When they cannot get along with people or make friends with others, they are setting their own traps.

3. Wallowing in self-pity creates self-bondage. Sometimes we dwell on self-pity without even knowing it. We lament that we were not born into a wealthy family or

were born at the wrong time. We may bear a grudge against a friend or family member for any wrongdoings or unkind words, or feel somehow that society has let us down. Worse still, we believe that the whole world is causing us trouble. In reality, if we fail to examine ourselves when faced with any difficulty but only blame the heavens or people around us, we are only binding ourselves. We cannot blame anyone but ourselves for our troubles.

4. Harboring anger produces enemies. The Buddhist scriptures teach, "As one thought of anger arises, a million gates of karmic obstruction open up," and "the fire of anger can burn up the forest of merits." When we often have hatred in our hearts, it is quite easy to get angry. Once anger arises, we will lose our reasoning and good sense, thereby creating many enemies for ourselves, which will lead to more obstructions and trouble. No matter how much merit we may have cultivated in ordinary times, all that we have achieved cannot overcome the fury of a single angry thought.

Hence, we should never set our own traps nor inflict troubles on ourselves. We need to pay attention to these tendencies in order to free ourselves.

Step Back and Ponder

In life, we have half the world in front of us and the other half behind us. Most people can only see what is in front and not behind them. Therefore, they fight with others everyday in the front half of the world until they are tired and battered. Yet, sometimes if we can step back and ponder, our perspective will be much broader and our world more open. In fact, "Step Back and Ponder" offers a profound philosophy of life.

1. It is better to be inarticulate than glib in argument. The greatest cultivation in life lies not in arguing with others. Some people like to argue and debate. They always want to get the upper hand and win an argument. In reality, the truth is not gained in being loud or expert with intellectual manipulation. If something is unreasonable, it does not matter how well you argue with a glib tongue; the truth will still not be on your side. On the other hand, those who are inarticulate and non-contentious are welcomed by others for their understanding and reason. Therefore, sometimes being inarticulate actually facilitates better reasoning.

2. It is better to be quiet than talkative. As the saying goes, "Actions speak louder than words." Being too talkative means one speaks when it is not appropriate or necessary to speak. There are people who like to talk, for when others say a few words, they can speak ten or twenty times as much. They may even carry on for twenty minutes nonstop. The truth is we make mistakes when we say too much. Being talkative not only earns the dislike of others but also results in creating grudges. The ancients treasured their speech like gold. The sayings

"Silence is golden," and "There is no danger as serious as talking too much" are certainly words of wisdom.

3. It is better to be opportune than rash. *Humble Table, Wise Fare* says, "No deluded thinking in the mind, no inappropriate action of the body and no improper speech from the mouth. The wise gain integrity as such." Some people like to show off and stand out in a group. They often act prematurely instead of waiting for matters to settle and conditions to ripen; consequently, their actions often result in failure. It is like singing, for if we are one beat ahead, we may drift out of tune. Therefore, we should always wait for the proper opportunities and conditions, instead of acting rashly when the timing is not right. Otherwise, we will find ourselves missing success and, as a result, wasting all our previous efforts. This means that we should resist acting impulsively and wait reasonably for a good opportunity to present itself.

4. It is better to be organized than chaotic. "With planning there will be no chaos; with job division there will be no rush." Some people are disorganized in their work and busy themselves without a clear sense of purpose. On other occasions they follow others in their mad rush, or worse still, the more they try to help, the more work they create for others. We should, however, be clear in our thinking and skillful in conducting ourselves at work. No matter how many things we are handling or how busy and chaotic the situation is, we should be organized. In other words, we should strive to find order in chaos, instead of running around blindly. Otherwise, we will achieve little despite our great efforts and lose the opportunity to learn from our work.

To step back and ponder is a way of thinking outside the box and resisting our impulsive ways. As we open up our mind, the world also opens up for us.

Making Gains

We all want to make gains in life. Children crave for more candy and farmers hope for a better harvest. Students want more encouragement and singers long for loud applause. Lovers seek commitment and practitioners hope for enlightenment to settle their mind. However, achievements do not fall from the sky, and we should not simply wait to see what others give us. The following are some proper ways of making gains:

1. Gain money through work. In modern society, money and finances are more important than anything else. If we do not have sufficient financial means, we will have trouble procuring our daily necessities even for a modest life style. Moreover, we also need funds if we want to practice some form of charity. *Humble Table, Wise Fare* reminds us, "Generosity is like planting seeds. By planting the seeds of positive conditions, we can reap the fruit." Likewise, if we want to make money, we cannot expect profit to come out of the blue. We must work hard at our career before we can make any gains!

2. Gain knowledge through learning. Wisdom is the navigator of life, and absorbing knowledge is the beginning of wisdom. "In the age of globalization, knowledge is the key and courage the attitude for success," claimed a contemporary management expert. Knowledge is the source of human motivation and the foundation for progress. However, knowledge does not mean merely embracing hearsay or repeating what we have heard. Knowledge is gained from diligent learning and raised to a higher level through critical thinking. Knowledge is like wealth accumulated slowly by saving dimes and

nickels over time. As long as we keep learning, our
knowledge will grow endlessly.

3. Gain experience through failures. Most people are afraid
   of failing because failure makes us lose self-confidence.
   In reality, failure is not to be feared, but we should fear
   losing hope, for if we fail, we can always try again.
   However, when we lose hope, we also lose our future.
   Failure is not completely negative. An enterprising person should have no fear of failures because he or she
   gains experience through them, transforming them into
   wisdom and eventually future success. Hence, "failure is
   the mother of success."

4. Gain merit through resolve. The best way to gain self-
   confidence is by our resolve, for it we can enhance ourselves and develop our potential. When we have resolve
   in walking, we can go very far. In having the resolve to
   eat, we can be truly satisfied. Similarly, we can sleep
   well only if we have the resolve to do so. We will gain
   success in whatever we do as long as we have resolve,
   because resolve gives us strength. The Buddhist scriptures teach us, "Merit is gained when our unwholesomeness ends; virtue is realized when our benevolence is
   perfect." This means our merits grow through our
   resolve in cultivation.

"The road seems to stop as the mountain and water appear
to end," but with perseverance we see "there is another village
behind the willows and flowers." "Wearing out shoes in climbing
to the cloud-covered the peak," but after the hard work we notice
"spring is already blooming from the branches." Farmers till in the
spring and cultivate in summer, and when they see the many grains
harvested at fall, they will smile and think, "Without the sweat of

planting seeds, how could there be a harvest of smiles?" Similarly, practitioners travel to different places to learn. When they make some gains in their mind-field, they will also say, "It was worth all the money spent on travel." After all, for whatever we seek to gain on the journey of life, we need to give something first.

Maintaining a Dignified Demeanor

There are all kinds of people in the world. Those who have money, have the appearance of wealth; those who have position, have the aura of power; and those who have knowledge, have the cultivation of the educated. The truth is, no matter what we have or do, we should all maintain a dignified demeanor. The following are some guidelines:

1. We need to cultivate honesty and righteousness. "The wise are righteous and honest; the crooked are always troubled and anxious." When we are righteous, then even though we may be ordinary, we will naturally be at ease and unaffected in our manners. This is the kind of cultivation we all should possess.

2. We need to have a broad and open heart. In conducting ourselves, we should all avoid having a narrow, selfish, and deluded mind. Otherwise, no one will like us, and we will find it difficult to reach out to the world. Therefore, we need to have a mind as broad as the ocean and as open as the sky.

3. We need proper poise and conduct. We do not necessarily have to be beautiful, elegant, or dashing. However, our manners should be proper and dignified, and we need to conduct ourselves with ease. Buddhism teaches, "Walk like the wind, sit like a bell, stand like a pine, and rest like a bow." Having appropriate manners and good poise are things we all should possess.

4. We need to speak compelling words of truth. While we need to teach with our actions, it is also important that we are articulate in guiding others towards the truth of the Dharma. If we cannot express ourselves properly, no one will be able to learn from us. Therefore, besides being learned, we must have the compassion and willingness to teach others the truth of the Dharma. When we speak, we should make a strong impression on others through the imminent truth of our words, so as to provide others with an affinity for the Dharma and thereby accept it with joy. Such is the cultivation we need.

While roses are beautiful, they do not last long. Therefore, while we may be good looking, we need to bring forth our dignified demeanor in order to connect well with others.

The Strength of Self-Control

We should have strength, but it does not mean we use it to punch or intimidate others. The greatest strength comes from within, for it is the strength of self-control and self-management. The following are some keys to self-control:

1. Do not be so biased as to confuse right with wrong. The ancients despised slanderers, coining the saying: "Slanderers ruin scholars" from the innumerable incidents of righteous scholars framed through slander. If we only believe what we hear and not use our eyes to observe, it will be easy for us to be deceived by the crooked. Many scams and hoaxes that exploit the biases of people appear in the media. This is why Buddhism stresses right belief in the Noble Eightfold Path, which comes from discerning the truth in what we hear by being mindful, non-judgmental, and thorough as listeners, for only then are we assured of making progress on the clear and correct track.

2. Do not act so impulsively as to be unstable. It is easy for us to indulge in our emotions by following our changing moods with little or no regard for circumstances. Some people do not rejoice or mourn with others when they should. In fact, their self-indulgence only reflects a lack of self-control and self-management. The Buddha taught his disciples "Not to get shot by the second arrow," meaning not creating more unwholesome karma from our ignorance and delusion because it will cause us even more suffering.

   The *Art of War* by Sunzi says, "A commander-in-chief cannot mobilize troops out of rage; a general cannot wage a war out of anger." Sunzi's attitude is wise and reasonable because if a battle is fought in anger, the strategy will probably be wrong and will result in a loss of too many lives. Therefore, we should never act on the impulse of anger.

3. Do not be so arrogant as to denigrate others. Some people consider themselves persuasive, capable, and resourceful, so they are arrogant and enjoy showing off their skills. However, they fail to realize that by being self-righteous and conceited, they are actually exposing their shortcomings. They forget the saying "heaven will not speak of its height nor earth its depth." The depth of "magnanimity" is profound indeed.

4. Do not be so ignorant as to envy the ability of others. Some incapable people are jealous of the capabilities of others. Consequently, they obstruct others from accomplishing things that they themselves cannot do. When they fail to make gains, they do not want others to benefit either. Such mentality lacks self-knowledge. Because of their jealousy of others' talents, they fail to learn from the experience of others and thus cannot gain anything themselves.

There are many examples in Chinese history where jealousy ended in tragedy. The great Legalist philosophers Hanfei and Li Si both fell victim to their mutual envy. On the other hand, Tang Dynasty poet Li Bai was generous in praising the work of his contemporaries and in so doing became a legend in history. These are indeed worthy lessons for future generations.

Confucianism teaches, "Self-control through reviving the rites." The strength of self-control leads to harmonious and peaceful exchanges in human relationships. We should therefore be mindful of our obstructive tendencies in nurturing self-control.

Capacity to Tolerate

According to the saying, "A lofty mountain does not reject any dirt, and so it can become high; the ocean does not shun small streams, and so it can become large." Likewise, in conducting ourselves and dealing with the world, we must have the capacity to tolerate others in order to lead them. "If the water is too clean, there will be no fish; if people scrutinize too closely, they will have no friends." "The wise treat others by following human sentiments. When people work for them, they will consider their strengths and not resent their shortcomings." All these sayings show that tolerance is a virtue and a noble characteristic, for in exercising our tolerance we are also cultivating our mind. The following verse offers an apt summary:

One can even ride a horse on the head of generals and ministers;
One can even row a boat in the belly of a lord.
Accept all kinds of grievances in the world;
Cultivate a sense of springtime within oneself.

The following explains the verse on the capacity to tolerate:

1. "One can even ride a horse on the head of generals and ministers:"

   People who want to achieve major accomplishments need to have the magnanimity and the capacity to tolerate. A leader with capacity will be able to bring together many people willing to work wholeheartedly for them. The Chinese Historian Ban Gu asserted, "If those ruling do not have the capacity to embrace their subjects, they should not hold the sacred positions." There are many examples in Chinese history when emperors did not dwell on past transgressions or insults of wise counselors, but instead relied on them to gain the throne or further their reign. Therefore, in addition to having knowledge and ability, it is even more important for rulers to have the magnanimity and the capacity to tolerate.

2. "One can even row a boat in the belly of a lord:"

A great person should be able to bend or be flexible, be big or small, and rise high or fall down. They have to embrace both the shortcomings and strengths of others. The founding emperor of the Han Dynasty, Liu Bang once stated, "I am not as good as Zi Fang in crafting victorious strategies and winning a battle a thousand miles away. I am not as skillful as Xiao He in administering the country and pacifying the citizens by providing them with supplies and money. I am not good in fighting like Han Xin who can lead a million troops and gain victory everywhere he goes. They all have outstanding talent, but when I can use them well, I can rule the land!" So people who want to make use of the strengths of others need to first learn to embrace them. Because Liu Bang had the capacity to do so, he was able to unify China.

3. "Accept all kinds of grievances in the world:"

Our capacity and cultivation can only be nurtured slowly through trials and tribulations. Therefore, even if we are wronged and abused by others, we have to accept them and should not bear any grudges. In fact, we have to embrace others and repay grievances with generosity and kindness, because only by doing so will our capacity grow over time. There is a story of a duke receiving as guests those who had unknowingly slaughtered his favorite horse. Another story recounts a king who condoned the attempts of a minister to seduce a favorite concubine. In both cases, they unwittingly saved their own lives in the end through their magnanimity.

4. "Cultivate a sense of springtime within oneself:"

As the Chan verse asserts, "When there is no attachment in our minds, even a small bed is wide; when we have sand in our eyes, even the whole universe seems narrow." When we can openly and completely accept the different climate of the four seasons, then all the beautiful vistas of spring, summer, autumn, and winter reside within our hearts. Even spring flowers and grass have to go through the heat of summer, the tempests and chill of autumn, and the cold and frost of winter before they can sprout and blossom again. Hence, even sages have to withstand hardships and obstacles in order to perfect their outstanding character.

Mencius said, "The benevolent are invincible." Benevolence signifies tolerance. The greater our tolerance, the more we can accomplish in our career and life in general. Hence, every great character must have the capacity to tolerate. We have to tolerate and embrace the strengths, shortcomings, merits, and faults of all kinds of people. When we can tolerate others, they will reciprocate, and our relationships will thrive.

The Beauty of Tolerance

In order to survive, we must bear many hardships in life including the various tests we have to face day to day due to our work and environment. It is only through the strength, wisdom, and courage of tolerance that we can resolve our difficulties and enhance our morals. The following are some definitions of the beauty of tolerance:

1. Tolerating hunger can reveal one's integrity. Since "People regard sustenance as heaven," food and water are essential for life. When people have to go hungry, it is the best time to measure their integrity. In Chinese history, there were examples of ministers who would rather starve to death than accept food from the enemy. As such, they made a clear statement of their integrity.

2. Tolerating poverty can eradicate one's greed. "Those who are well-fed and well-clad are inclined to be lustful, whereas hunger and cold breed the temptation to steal." Some poor people become greedy when they observe the wealth of others. Hence, they kill, steal, or rob, committing crimes because they cannot tolerate poverty. Yet, if they can live a life of simplicity and find contentment in what they have, then they will not be so greedy as to engage in crime. Therefore, tolerating poverty can rid oneself of greed.

3. Tolerating indignities can enhance morals. It is easier for us to accomplish the feats of tolerating hunger, frost, poverty, or suffering. However, it is difficult to tolerate indignities, because it demands so much more inner cul-

tivation. If we can restrain our temper and keep calm in the face of wrongs, setbacks, and hurts, accepting them willingly instead of being petty, we will enhance our morals.

4. Tolerating insults can strengthen one's fortitude. When others hurt and insult us, but we have the strength to bear it, we can then shoulder almost any major responsibility. If friends or subordinates are able to tolerate insults and take on serious responsibilities, we can safely put them in charge of major undertakings. No matter how difficult the task, those who have fortitude can help us carry the load.

Therefore, tolerance is strength, wisdom, and courage. It is taking on responsibilities and understanding life. People who are able tolerate conditions and the behavior of others can truly enjoy peace in their life.

The Way of Humility

In getting along with others, a humble attitude is key. A stalk of ripe wheat inevitably lowers its top, and likewise a mature person always treats others with deference. A philosopher once proclaimed, "How high is the universe? Only five feet." It is high enough to accommodate people six-foot tall, but easier if they lower their heads a little. Therefore, in conducting ourselves, we must appreciate the way of humility. The following are a few guidelines on being humble:

1. Treating our seniors with respect and humility is a matter of course. We all have parents, teachers, seniors, and elders, and we naturally have to be respectful of them. As Confucius who asserted, "When there are food and drinks, teachers eat; when there is work, students serve." Therefore, being filial towards our parents and humble towards our seniors is a matter of course for how we conduct ourselves.

2. Treating friends and associates with humility is kindness. In dealing with our friends, coworkers, classmates, and associates, we need to be humble. We should pay them respect and put them in a higher position than our own as a sign of our amity and kindness. When we treat others with humility, we will make good connections with them, and they will in turn find it easy to accept us and work with us.

3. Treating juniors and subordinates with humility is nobleness. When relating to people from a younger generation, such as nephews, nieces, students, or subordinates,

we should not be arrogant and place ourselves in a higher position. However, being humble does not mean lowering ourselves or making ourselves any less worthy. On the contrary, it displays a noble character which will win the respect of others even more.

4. Treating strangers with humility is security. Sometimes, we come across people we do not know well. Whether it is from work, through the introduction of another person, or just someone we meet by chance, it is always safer for us to be humble and deferential in dealing with such people. If we treat someone with contempt only to find out later that he or she is our superior, the consequences of putting ourselves in such an awkward position are obvious. Clearly then, it is always safer to treat strangers with humility.

All matters succeed because of humility, and failures are caused by arrogance. Therefore, we need to be humble. Like the good earth with its inclusive magnanimity, humility can hold all matters and support all accomplishments. Hence, we should be mindful of the above in practicing the way of humility.

Our Practice

We go through life first pursuing an education followed by establishing our career. But we need to cultivate our virtues and improve our practice throughout our life. Our practice in life involves school, work, and ethics, through which we learn to rectify our conduct, enhance our intelligence and skills, and establish our merit in life. We should gradually keep improving our knowledge, morals, and conduct so that we are not wasting precious time. The following are some ways to approach our practice:

1. Have faith in ourselves. The worst thing to lose is our self-confidence. People lacking self-confidence cannot inspire faith or hope in others. Worse still, those who are unsure of themselves will find it difficult to gain the approval of others. Therefore, we must have faith in ourselves and know clearly our strengths and shortcomings. By knowing ourselves clearly, we will be able to develop our future.

2. Nurture a passion for our profession. We all wish to succeed in our career and keep growing and improving, and perhaps even becoming wealthier over time. Regardless of our profession, if we do not strive with passion, nor have any sense of mission or interest in our work, we will not be able to do well in our career. Therefore, a passion for work is of prime importance in every field. When we accept our job as a part of life and maintain our interest and enthusiasm, not only will time pass swiftly, but the meaning of life will also be enriched.

3. Exhibit diligence for learning. We should never stop

learning in life. Even teachers and principals of schools are learning as they teach, because the two pursuits actually complement each other. Even as teachers, we must have the intention to explore, do research, and seek endless new knowledge. Sometimes when we are teaching others, we can gain new experience from our students. Thus, "Never tire of teaching; never become weary of learning" is the right attitude in academic pursuits.

4. Gain realizations in our practice. Every religion in the world has its special emphasis of practice. Confucius and Mencius both advocated self-reflection and the cultivation of integrity. Likewise, we also need moments of realization and affirmation in our practice, where we can feel we are beginning to understand the true nature of things. Such realizations allow us to fully integrate our practice into our body and mind. Only then will we have the necessary resources to advance our practice.

Practitioners

Practicing Buddhism involves application, cultivation, and actualization. In other words, it should correct and improve our behavior. In most religions, followers are required to pursue both faith and practice in the teachings. Likewise in Buddhism, practitioners seek to realize the state of enlightenment achieved by the Buddha. In diligently learning and practicing the Dharma, they are considered "practitioners." Generally speaking, some people only view monastics as practitioners. However, members of the laity, certain vegetarians, and the wise and virtuous who are ethical and compassionate are also called practitioners. The following are a few definitions of practitioners:

1. People who teach others the Law of Cause and Effect are practitioners. A person may not need to believe in all Buddhist teachings, but he or she must appreciate the meaning of cause and effect. "Wholesome behavior brings good effects; unwholesome behavior brings bad results. It is not that there is no retribution; it is only a matter of time." The cause and effect of wholesome and unwholesome behavior are very scientific realities. If we have a clear understanding of the Law of Cause and Effect, we will not easily commit any evil deed or unwholesome act. Thus, we will certainly not ruin our lives nor contribute to social disorder. Therefore, people who teach others the Law of Cause and Effect are practitioners.

2. People who alleviate the difficulties of others are practitioners. If we help others solve their problems when they are in trouble and suffering, we are sharing their burden. Furthermore, when others have too many worries and

attachments in their mind, we can counsel them. We have to use the wisdom of the Dharma so that they can liberate themselves from the bondage of ignorance and defilements. Such is the conduct of a practitioner.

3. People who shoulder the suffering of others are practitioners. Some people can only share in the fortune of others but not in their pain. A practitioner on the other hand should provide assistance to others in times of trouble. For instance, we can offer others some helpful conditions or spend time with them to show them support. When others are down and feel sad, we can offer them a smile or some words of encouragement, so as to pull them out of the pit of depression. This is also a form of practice.

4. People who delight in the joy of others are practitioners. It is rare for people to willingly go through suffering with others. Likewise, it is rare for people to share in the joy of others. However, if we put on a sad face when others are happy, not only do we suffer but we also ruin their joy. Therefore, when others are doing well and enjoying themselves, we should never spoil their good time, by being envious or spiteful. We need to take joy in the moment and offer praise and congratulation. As practitioners, we must be able to support others in good times and share in the joy and harmony.

Practice is not necessarily based on how many Buddhist sutres we recite, how many bows we make, or how many charitable acts we do everyday. The key lies in our daily living, where we can regularly perform kind deeds, speak joyful words, and have positive thoughts. The best approach to practice is following conditions in helping others and providing assistance whenever we can.

The Mind of a Practitioner

There are many religions in the world today, and no matter what religion we follow, we all need to practice well. A practitioner must have the will and mind to do so, because if we are practitioners in name only, our religion would just be an empty label. What is the mind of a practitioner? The following are some definitions:

1. Adopt a non-discriminating mind of the Middle Way in dealing with human sentiments. In life, the love and emotions between people can be strong at times and weak at others. Sometimes, people treat us very well, showering us with endearments, while at other times, they are distant and cool. Tossed in between the warm and cold sentiments, some people will become anxious about where they stand. Therefore, they will be easily bound by emotions. If we can maintain the non-discriminating mind of the Middle Way, we will not be bothered by either the strong or weak emotions that others express.

2. Adopt a non-anxious mind of acceptance in dealing with the flux in life. Success and failure are inevitable in life. Some people rejoice when things are going well and brood when faced with setbacks. Their rejection of difficulties demonstrates that they do not have the strength to overcome hardship and worry. Moreover, they do not have the cultivation to handle success either. Therefore, they end up being tossed in the constant flux of life. If we have the non-anxious mind of acceptance in dealing with both success and failure, we will be like Maitreya Bodhisattva who puts everything that is both good and

bad in his wondrous bag. What ease! Hence, if we want to be as liberated and tranquil as this bodhisattva, we must have a mind of acceptance unaffected by changing circumstances.

3. Adopt a non-attached mind of equanimity in dealing with sorrow and joy. Ups and downs, sorrow and joy, are all realities of life. When we are neither devastated by sorrow nor indulgent in joy, our mind will rest in equanimity. If we are able to dissolve any positive or negative emotion, we would have attained the mind of a practitioner.

4. Adopt a non-calculating mind of fairness in dealing with gain and loss. Many people live each day calculating their gains and losses. They either dwell on how much money or property they have gained, or they think about how much others like or dislike them. They are tossed endlessly in the cycle of profit and loss, never knowing contentment. We should appreciate that what we have is not our possession, but commonly owned by all, and that not having is just as good as having. After all, "emptiness" is limitlessness and boundlessness, so not having can mean having more. By being able to be non-calculating and fair, we can be one with the Way.

Therefore, a practitioner must be able to deal with all positive and negative matters in life with a mind of the Middle Way, acceptance, equanimity, and fairness.

How to Cultivate

"It takes ten years to cultivate a tree and a hundred years a person." Over the ages, Eastern and Western cultures have both been bent on cultivating human resources. During the Warring States Period, Meng Changjun of the Qi State supported many scholars and talented people numbering several thousand. He was cultivating human resources. How do we cultivate? The following are some guidelines:

1. Cultivate the roots in planting trees. No matter how tall trees grow, they cannot do without their roots. If the roots are rotting, nutrients cannot be absorbed and no leaves, flowers, or fruit can flourish. Therefore, in cultivating trees and plants, we must nurture them from the roots and not just tend to the leaves and stems. We cannot ignore the roots because they are buried in the ground and out of our sight. As long as the roots are intact, even a fallow field can flourish once again. The roots of plants are like the teaching of cause and effect in Buddhism. Everything in the world originates from a root or cause. Therefore, in conducting ourselves, we need to "stand firm on the roots of our feet." Likewise, in solving problems, we have to explore these roots. We can blossom and bear fruit when we have roots, or else we are just like duckweed floating everywhere, always finding it difficult to settle down and establish ourselves.

2. Cultivate the mind in nurturing morals. The Buddhist scriptures teach, "If one does not one's mind, there is no benefit in learning the Dharma." The mind is like a spring, for when the source is clean, the stream will be clear. Therefore, the wise and virtuous over the ages

have emphasized the importance of cultivating mind and nature. The mind is the master of all conduct. Like the multi-layered petals of a flower, the many layers do not depart from the center. The *Platform Sutra of the Sixth Patriarch* also indicates, "All fields of merit do not abandon the mind-field." When we guard our every thought well, our conduct will develop on the right track. Thus, in cultivating the blossoms of morality, we must start from the mind so that what we say can spread fragrance far and wide.

3. Cultivate breadth in nurturing capacity. "One can even row a boat in the belly of a lord." However, there are people who "will not pluck a single hair of their own even if it would be of benefit to the world." In reality, sharing food with a group will make it taste so much better. Laozi asserted, "Supreme benevolence is like water. Water benefits all things and does not contend." This is the best metaphor for capacity. Buddhas and bodhisattvas alike have "Minds like the cosmos encompassing realms as numerous as grains of sand." Because they hold limitless sentient beings within their minds, they are able to perfect the path of bodhisattva practice. Large fields of wheat and flowers are especially attractive and pleasing to the both eyes and the heart. Our life experiences also need to be passed on, but in order to fully embrace and benefit the world, we must have the capacity to teach others just like Buddhas and bodhisattvas.

4. Cultivate diligence in nurturing merit. The causes and conditions of our merit and fortune are not heaven sent, nor do they develop merely through the love and support of our parents and teachers. A mansion starts from a brick and an embroidered garment from a thread.

Likewise, our accomplishments depend on our diligence and hard work. We reap what we sow, and nurturing merit is like developing a field. We must toil with our hands and feet to cultivate diligently before we can succeed. It is only through hard work that we can fully appreciate and treasure the harvest we earn.

A country's culture needs to be supported and encouraged and its social systems carefully developed to enhance and protect the lives of its citizens. Nowadays, research in science has discovered that genes can be changed through cultivation. Hence, when we are willing to use care in cultivation, the future holds endless hope. We should pay attention to the above guidelines.

The Way to Cultivate

We need to have cultivation, because only cultivated people can gain the respect of others. Cultivation is the reason for us to become educated, seek knowledge, and broaden our vistas. Cultivated people have reasoning, etiquette, respect, and humility, and their every gesture tells others how polished they are. The following are some guidelines on how to cultivate oneself:

1. Deep water allows ships to sail. We can test someone's cultivation with words and the depth of water with a pole. When the water is deep enough, ships can sail. All the commercial and naval ports in the world have standard depths for military ships and commercial liners to dock. Likewise, only deep water can nurture big fish. If we cultivate ourselves to be like deep harbors, all our friends will be able to count on us. If we can show the depth of our cultivation with how we speak and act, we can win the respect of others.

2. Calm water shows clarity. When a stone is thrown in water, there will be ripples, and when there is wind, there will be waves. We are often like water in conducting ourselves, for when obstacles arise, we often cannot reason and remain clear-headed. We lose control in dealing with circumstances when we get blown by the winds of delusion. Yet, when the waves are gone and the water is calm, we can again see our own reflection. We can easily lose sight of our true self when there are waves in the lake of our mind. Hence, our level of cultivation needs to withstand obstacles, temptations, or provocation. If we can remain calm in face of any disruption, we will be like a calm lake. When the water is calm, our reasoning

will be clear, and our mind will not blindly respond to changing circumstances.

3. Simplicity brings calmness. Some people live a hectic life and may actually feel awkward when their mind quiets down. They tend to enjoy the hustle bustle and do not cherish simplicity. In reality, simplicity can calm us, and calmness can simplify our life. When we appreciate a simple life, we can truly live life by enjoying its quiet moments. When life is simple, nobody will be jealous of us; when we live life quietly, no one will find us offensive. Therefore, only simplicity and calmness can show us the true meaning of life. Once we gain a sense of order in life, we will be able to organize well and rest our body and mind. Chan Buddhism teaches, "We only need a ladle to taste the water in the ocean." This means in facing the myriad colors of the world and the temptations of sensual pleasures, we need to have mindfulness and a calm mind. With such cultivation, life will indeed be beautiful.

4. By trimming and polishing, we create a useful vessel. "Jade must be cut and chiseled to make it a useful vessel; a person must be disciplined and educated to be righteous." Our cultivation cannot be completed in a day. It needs to withstand the trials and tribulations of life over time. "Jade needs the polish of deft hands; gold requires the tempering of the fiery furnace." Without the test of hardships and going through endless births and deaths, how can there be any hope of success? Therefore, true cultivation is not to be taken lightly, nor can it be achieved from being idle. We must have confidence and perseverance to go through life and death in order to succeed.

Therefore, through cultivation we find the value of life and the prescription for conducting ourselves and dealing with matters.

Key to Cultivation

We often hear people say, "Cultivate the mind, and nurture our nature." While the mind certainly needs cultivation, the rest of our sense organs – eyes, ears, mouth, as well as every one of our limbs – should also be trained. Hence, the key to cultivation does not apply just to the mind. We need to cultivate both our body and mind, both the external and the internal. The following are some guidelines for doing so:

1. A face without anger is a true offering. Buddhism advocates making offerings. Devotees often make ten offerings to the buddhas and bodhisattvas, which include incense, flowers, lamps, oil, fruit, tea, food, treasure, beads, and clothing. But the best offering we can make does not necessarily entail material things. People may offer money, fruits, or special gifts. However, if they make an offering without sincerity or a true heart, but do so instead with a stern face, it will become meaningless. On the other hand, nothing can compare to the joy of an honest and true smile given to others, because such a smile is the most welcoming sight. Who in the world would not wish for a smile from others? Therefore, a face without anger is the best offering.

2. A mouth of praise is wondrous incense. This is the age that focuses so much on sights and sounds. So besides keeping a smile on our face, we should also sing often the song of praise. Radio and television stations nowadays are very serious about the quality of their sound. Some stereo systems can deliver very high-quality digital sound, but may cost thousands of dollars, while a small boom box may be cheaper, but the sound is often

far less rich to our ears. Likewise, the sounds people make with their mouths can be either pleasing or jarring. Some people, as soon as they open their mouths, make demeaning remarks about others. Others sound like music from heaven or smell like fragrant flowers whenever they speak. People's hearts also blossom when they listen to them talk. If we can speak in a way that gives others joy and make them happy, then our words will be more meaningful and, thus become the best offering we can make.

3. A compassionate mind is invaluable treasure. Most people's minds are filled with greed, anger, and delusion. Therefore, we have to cultivate our mind. How do we do that? It is most important to cultivate compassion. Buddhism sees "compassion as the basis; skillful means as the gate." The meaning of compassion is giving joy and alleviating suffering. Being able to bring others joy and uproot their suffering is the most invaluable way to cultivate ourselves.

4. Buddha's light brings incomparable fortune, longevity, and good health. People often ask, "Where is the Buddha?" The Buddha is in the Pure Land of Everlasting Light, the World of Ultimate Bliss, and in the universe. These are all correct answers. However, in learning the Dharma, what is most important is to cultivate the Buddha in our mind and in our hearts. If we have the Buddha in our mind, we can feel his existence and share in the Dharma body of the Buddha all the time. This is what we mean by "the Buddha's light shines universally for all." As such, we can naturally gain fortune, longevity, peace, and good health.

Therefore, it is best for us to cultivate and use all our six sense organs at the same time.

Cultivating Ourselves in the Midst of Life

Most people have misconceptions about cultivation. They think that it entails either reciting Buddhist sutras or making bows to the Buddha in the shrine hall. Or else, they assume it means living like a hermit deep in the mountains, completely detached from the mundane world. In reality, according to the Sixth Patriarch Huineng, "The Dharma is in the world and not apart from worldly matters. Seeking enlightenment away from the world is like looking for horns on a rabbit." True cultivation begins with how we conduct ourselves and deal with situations in our daily life. We are cultivating ourselves when we treat others with compassion, shoulder responsibilities, conduct ourselves with ease and poise, and get along well with people. Cultivation is not a mere mantra or ritual. When our conduct naturally conveys morals, abides with the Middle Way, shows compassion for all sentient beings, we are truly cultivating ourselves. But if we detach ourselves from life and the world, there is no cultivation whatsoever. How do we cultivate ourselves in the world? The following are some guidelines:

1. Learn to speak kind words. According to a saying, "Kind words can be spoken a thousand times." If we want to succeed in life or achieve our goals at work, we need to speak more kind words. Actually, no matter what we do or with whom we interact, we also need to cultivate positive speech. There is nobody in the world who does not like to hear kind words spoken. Speaking gently actually allows us to become a kinder person and do more kind deeds. In turn, others will naturally grow fonder of us and notice our good deeds. Therefore, we need to praise, encourage, and respect others more in how we speak. There are actually never enough kind words. Sometimes, it is even a virtue to utter words of praise just to boost the confidence of those who need it.

2. Learn to care. In addition to speaking kind words, we also need to take action with our true heart in caring for others. For instance, we can provide support for people who are not strong enough, donate resources for those in poverty, teach those who lack knowledge, and pass on some skills to those who lack them. We show compassion and enhance our own cultivation when we care for others.

3. Learn to interact well. We may be very learned and knowledgeable, yet still foolish and ignorant if we do not know how to interact well with people. In conducting ourselves, we need to show tact in our conduct, and finesse in sensing when to advance or retreat. When others provide us with benefits, we should reciprocate with twice as much. When others praise us, we should bestow on them twice as many words of praise. If people smile at us once, we need to smile back two or three times. People who can interact well with others will inevitably enjoy harmonious human relationships.

4. Learn to be patient. Patience is the greatest strength in life. It can tap into our mind's inner power. With that strength, we will not be easily deluded, distracted, or flustered. Instead, the more setbacks we face, the more courageous we can be in overcoming them. In the end, patience breeds wisdom. When we can view all phenomena in the world with wisdom, then naturally there will not be anything worth getting angry over. Patience is thus the greatest cultivation.

These four lessons should remind us that true Buddhist cultivation takes place in the midst of the mundane world.

Cultivating the Six Roots

We often hear people say, "We need to cultivate our mind and nurture our nature." Actually, cultivating our mind alone is not enough. Our six roots or sense organs – eyes, ears, nose, tongue, body, and mind – are always in contact with the "six dusts" latching on the external conditions that keep tempting us to commit all kinds of unwholesome karma. Therefore, the Buddhist scriptures describe the six roots as six robbers constantly stealing the merits of our cultivation. How do we avoid the harm that our six roots may cause us? We must cultivate them well. The following are some guidelines in doing so:

1. Use our eyes to see our own shortcomings. Most people use their eyes to look for the faults in others, but not their own inadequacies. Therefore, they dislike everyone they see. If we can change our view and examine ourselves as to our own shortcomings and mistakes, we are cultivating our eyes.

2. Use our ears to hear disagreeable words. According to the saying, "Good medicine is bitter for the mouth; sound advice is grating to the ears." Most people's ears can only hear words of praise and positive things about themselves. However, they are oblivious to the sincere counsel of friends or may even get upset on hearing them. If we are willing to accept the advice of others or even be happy in learning about our own faults, we are cultivating our ears.

3. Use our nose to smell the fragrance of the wise and holy. Our nose can seek out fragrance or detect odors. It is like

an intelligence agent on the pursuit. Our nose is indeed very sensitive. However, most people's noses are busy pursuing the aromas of food and drink. If we can instead detect the fragrance of the wise and holy, we are cultivating our nose.

4. Use our tongue to taste the flavor of the truth. Being able to sample the tastes of gourmet food in the world is considered a great fortune. However, "sickness enters through the mouth; trouble comes out of the mouth." This is common knowledge we all appreciate. Hence, it is best for our tongue to truly appreciate the taste of the Dharma. Moreover, we should develop ourselves in how we propagate the truth of the Dharma with our mouth. This is what is meant by the cultivation of our tongue.

5. Use our body to come into contact with purity. Our body prefers comfortable temperatures and likes things which are gentle and soft to the touch. Therefore, we rest on soft velvety sofas, sleep on soft mattresses, and enjoy air-conditioning during heat waves and in-door heating during cold winter months. If we can go to a temple from time to time to meditate, honor the Buddha, walk straight, and sit upright, allowing our bodies to come into contact with a quiet and spiritual environment, we can cultivate our body.

6. Use our mind to think of the joy emanating from compassion and harmony. There is a saying, "If people are not selfish, even heaven and earth would damn them." Most people only think of how they can make a profit, become famous, hit the jackpot, or succeed in whatever they are scheming. Actually, we need to think of how to become more compassionate and just, work for peace,

and help others. It is especially important for us to commit ourselves to "alleviating the suffering of sentient
beings and not focusing on pursuing our own peace and
joy." Such is the cultivation of the mind.

Cultivation is not just lip service or a mere thought. We
are not just saying it for the benefit of others. It is an honest and
realistic practice and application. In cultivation, we need not even
discuss liberation from rebirth. What we need is to first cultivate
our six roots well because by doing so, we will receive endless
merit.

Cultivating Body and Mind

When our clothes are torn, we need to mend them. When our house leaks, we have to repair it, and when our body and mind are sick, we also need to cure them. How do we heal our body and mind? We must cultivate and maintain their well being at ordinary times. The following are keys to cultivating the body and mind:

1. Watch over our body like jade. People all like things that are clean. For instance, clean clothes are comfortable to put on, fresh food is healthy to eat, and a hygienic environment is pleasant to live in. Similarly, by safeguarding our body like jade, we gain the respect and company of others. If we want our body to be pristine like a piece of fine jade with no blemishes, we have to cultivate it by not killing, not stealing, and not engaging in sexual misconduct.

2. Keep our mouth tight like a sealed bottle. "Sickness comes in through the mouth; trouble comes out of it." Our mouth creates much trouble for us because we like to talk. Many disasters are the result of inappropriate speech. Therefore, we should not say anything improper because what we say needs to be acceptable and beneficial to others. Otherwise, our words will only bring many undesirable consequences.

3. Guard our mind like thieves. Ming scholar Wang Yangming asserted, "It is easy to capture the bandit in the mountain but difficult to catch the thief in the mind." The Buddhist scriptures compare our body to a village with six thieves within – eyes, ears, nose, tongue, body,

and mind, with mind being the leader. It leads our eyes, ears, nose, tongue, and body in committing unwholesome deeds and disrupting our life so that we can never find peace. Therefore, if we want to live in peace and harmony, we must guard against this bandit called the "mind" and not allow it to offend anyone or create disorder.

4. Eradicate evil like an enemy. The Buddhist scriptures state that body, speech, and mind are the masterminds behind our every deed. They can lead us to practice benevolence or commit unwholesome deeds. It often happens that whether a deed is kind or evil is determined by a single thought. In eradicating the unwholesome deeds from our body, speech, and mind, we need a sharp sword of wisdom. Thus, we must view sins as bandits and foes in order to stamp them out.

We must pay attention to the above admonitions in cultivating our body and mind.

Cultivation for Lay People

We all need to cultivate because cultivation is not the monopoly of monastics. Lay people living at home can also practice the Dharma. They do not necessarily have to go to temples to practice because their homes are already good places in which to do so. The following are some guidelines on cultivation for members of the laity:

1. Honor our parents and practice filial piety in the best possible way. Respecting our seniors and practicing filial piety by honoring and caring for our parents are the most important ways to cultivate at home. According to the saying, "If we do not even honor our parents at home, what is the merit in paying homage to the Buddha in a temple faraway?" Our parents are our fields of merit in this life. They are like Buddhas and bodhisattvas, beings we should honor and respect. If we do not even practice filial piety, others will certainly doubt our sincerity when we tell them we are respectful of the Buddha and want to serve all sentient beings.

2. Consistently teach our relatives benevolence. In getting along with members of our family, relatives, and associates, we need to apply ethics, compassion, loving-kindness, and the truth of cause and effect. We have to influence them with these positive concepts so that they will be able to live and act benevolently and not digress onto the wrong path. Otherwise, they may live in endless remorse for taking a wrong step because it will be very difficult for them to turn back.

3. Be kind to those working for us and know their needs. We may have help at home and employees in our businesses. We must protect and care for them, especially knowing what their needs are. If we are able to resolve difficulties for our staff when they have problems with their livelihood, they will certainly work for us more wholeheartedly. On the other hand, if we are unable to provide them with proper assistance when needed, then they may be with us in body only, because their heart will not be there, thus failing them as their leader. Hence, caring for people who work for us and knowing their needs are forms of cultivation.

4. Draw closer to benevolent friends and distance ourselves from unwholesome people. In our daily life, we have to get acquainted with wholesome people and learn from them. "One who nears vermilion becomes red; one who nears ink becomes black." On the journey of life, we will not be waylaid if we have the support of wholesome friends. Moreover, we need to become a good friend ourselves by counseling others to practice kindness and not commit any evil.

"The Dharma is to be found in the human world; it is not removed from worldly matters." True cultivation needs to be realized and applied in daily living. The above guidelines can be used for cultivation as a layperson.

The Standards for Cultivation

"First cultivate oneself, then bring order to the family and the state, and peace to the world" is a core teaching of the Confucian School that underscores the primary importance of moral cultivation. When one's personal morality is cultivated, the family will be regulated; when the family is regulated, the state will be in order; and when the state is in order, there will be peace in the world. Cultivation is emphasized by all the world's major religions because it can cleanse one's impurities, develop open-mindedness, and nurture the integrity for wholesome behavior. Buddhism teaches us "to abide in the Buddha and perfect our moral character." In emulating the Buddha's spirit, we must first learn to have self-restraint, propriety, self-discipline, and morality in order to fully develop the light of wisdom. Throughout history, others have emulated the cultivation of the virtuous and the moral standards they had set. The following are four effects of cultivation:

1. Cultivation leads to a noble temperament. While money can buy beautiful clothes and expensive cosmetics, it cannot improve a person's disposition which comes from moral cultivation. "Those who wish to cultivate themselves must first rectify their minds," as stated in *The Great Learning*, a Confucian classic on the importance of virtue. To rectify the mind is to overcome delusion and exercise self-discipline. We also need to nurture our temperament with propriety. As Confucius taught, "Do not look at, listen to, or talk about what is improper; never commit to action that which is not in accordance with the rules of propriety." Consequently, we should be dignified in our demeanor, cultivated in our manners, and distinguished in our disposition.

2. Cultivation leads to a dignified poise. How do we know if a person's words and deeds are careful and sincere? How do we know if a person's conduct is without flaw or complaint? The answer lies in their standard for self-cultivation. Confucius said, "With sincerity within, one will naturally appear sincere." In order for us to be dignified and poised in our bearing, we must be kind, patient, and tolerant. During the Three Kingdoms Period, the renowned strategist Zhuge Liang said, "one should not laugh uncontrollably when one is happy; one should not go stamping around when one is angry; one should not cry loudly from abandonment when one is sad; and one should not be frivolous when one is pleased." These are the proper actions of a person who is wise and poised.

3. Cultivation leads to a more approachable demeanor. In today's society, a person can only gain the goodwill and support of others through a self-effacing and humble demeanor. Such approachable demeanor is neither scornful nor flattering; thus, it can win friendships by bridging gaps between people and building a positive network of interpersonal relationships. As such, an approachable demeanor is a reflection of cultivation and the guiding principle of conduct in this world.

4. Cultivation leads to the Middle Way. It is imperative for us to be neither biased nor obstinate, neither condescending nor haughty. In cultivating inner peace and living a life of true freedom, our mind must be pure and tranquil, active and optimistic. We must not be bothered by gossip or slander, nor seduced by worldly desires. *The Analects* teaches, "Those who are benevolent and virtuous are kind without expectation, diligent without complaint, poised without arrogance, dignified without

dominance, and enjoy pleasure without greed." With such cultivation, our conduct would be unhurried and our attitude peaceful.

As the saying goes, "It is better to find help in forming connections with others; it is better to seek good fortune in cultivating oneself." The above guidelines clearly underscore the importance of cultivation.

Learning and Practicing Together

Learning and practicing are life-long endeavors for each of us. Sometimes we have to learn and practice on our own, but many times we do so with others. On an individual level, we schedule our own learning and choose the areas for our own personal and discreet practice. However, in learning and practicing with others, we have to reconcile our schedule with that of everyone else so that we can study and support one another. The following are some views on learning and practicing together with others:

1. While we can take an individual approach, it is more important to connect with a community. Humans cannot live alone nor indulge in vanity. Although each of us should spend time alone everyday, we need to spend more time being with a community, especially when it comes to learning and practicing. We should not engage in solipsistic practice aimed only towards self-liberation. Instead, we should interact with others and be part of a group. Hence, Buddhism advocates group practice and activities, meaning we have to share our practice with other devotees and be a member of the lay community.

2. While we may function on our own, it is more important to value teamwork. In working on our own, each person shoulders tasks on their own at all levels. But even when taking on responsibilities individually, one still needs the support and assistance of the group. Therefore, we have to cooperate well with others while working on our own schedule. When we are able to work well in both ways, we can take full advantage of the benefits of joint effort, so that by working as a team we can accomplish greater undertakings. Temples and monasteries interact with

other faiths and orders in order to learn from each other. In our personal cultivation and learning, we also need many Dharma friends coming together to study and review what we have been learning. Hence, while there needs to be some division of responsibilities, cooperation with a group is also important.

3. While we all have human feelings, it is more important to observe social morals. In dealing with issues, we cannot depart from our feelings, reasoning, and the law. Sometimes, as long as they do not compromise the welfare of the community, we can have our own views, characteristics, and needs. In fact, once in a while, we may even follow our spontaneous feelings in doing someone a favor. However, "An old monk would rather fall into hell than use the Dharma as a favor." When we are facing the truth of the Dharma or social justice, we need to have moral courage and look after the welfare of the community. We must have social morals, and community service and interaction instead of focusing on personal needs or feelings. Acting this way, we will be able to accomplish more on the path of our cultivation.

4. While there should be internal or personal cultivation, it is more important to establish external conditions. Some people only concentrate on their own practice and refuse to help or make connections with others. As such, they may be able to be highly cultivated, let go of all attachments, and give up all worldly desires and cravings. However, they lack the external conditions to support them, enabling them to create strong connections with others. As a result, they may not be welcomed or liked by people wherever they go. This is not true cultivation, since according to a Buddhist saying, "Before one attains

Buddhahood, one needs first to make connections with people." As humans, we cannot survive on our own. Therefore, we have to nurture many external causes and conditions, because it is through them that we can survive.

It is inevitable that sometimes we will get lazy. By learning and practicing together with others, we can make use of the strength of the group to motivate us. External conditions can lend us the discipline and tempering so we will not slack off. The benefits of learning and practicing together can be compared to that of burning a fire. With one log, the fire is small, but with many logs, the fire can blaze bright and hot. It is also like hitting something with one finger, for the impact is very limited, but if we form a fist with all our fingers, the punch is much stronger. Therefore, learning and practicing together as a group is very important for us Buddhists.

The Resolve of the Virtuous

"If we do not commit any deeds in life that others frown upon, no one in the world would gnash their teeth." The nobleness of a person's character can be observed over time because time is the best testimony for morals. A virtuous and ethical person has a distinctive attitude toward life and a different sense of morals and integrity from that of others. The following are some definitions of the resolve of the virtuous:

1. Slander or praise cannot affect the resolve of people with self-confidence. We must have self-confidence because only we can be our own master when we are sure of ourselves. When we have confidence in our conduct, career, country, and society, we will not be moved by the praise, ridicule, honor, or defamation from the outside world. We will not be angry when libeled or buoyed when praised. People with self-confidence can transcend both the insults and laurels from others. Hence, regardless of how others look at them, they will not change their original vow and compromise their resolve.

2. Power cannot alter the integrity of people who are content. Contentment is the greatest possession in life. We can be content with the status of our position or with the amount of money we own, no matter how insignificant these may be. Even the strongest power cannot move people who are happy with what they have in their life. Their integrity will not be affected by the pressure of power or the temptation of profit. Such is the will of people who are content.

3. Gratitude and ill-will cannot move the spirit of people who are tranquil. People cultivated in meditative concentration have a tranquil mind. They will not be easily agitated by what others say or do because of their calmness. Hence, the spirit of people with a calm mind will not be stirred by gratitude, ill-will, kindness or evil. Their spiritual world will not be affected by external circumstances due to their inner cultivation.

4. Gossip cannot disturb the mind of people with virtue. While the world may be filled with gossip or conflict between people, the virtuous will not be affected. Why is this so? They never speak, listen to, or spread gossip. Furthermore, they have no fear for gossip. So even though storms may be brewing in the outside world and life is rife with gossip, they will only look upon them as illusions. Nothing can disturb their mind.

Therefore, we should all learn from the resolve of the virtuous.

The Sublime Uses of the Four Immeasurables

In Buddhism, loving-kindness, compassion, sympathetic joy, and equanimity are four states of mind referred to as the "Four Immeasurables." Since their cultivation is necessary for improving interpersonal relationships, how do we bring their sublime uses into full play? The following are some keys to consider:

1. Loving-kindness can overcome brutality. The *Avadana Sutra* teaches, "Never repay hatred with hatred, if we want to put an end to the cycle of revenge." It is best to avoid unnecessary confrontations when we come across unreasonable and violent types. An angry stare or a threat of violence will only serve to further antagonize our foes and force us into a no-win situation. On the other hand, if we counter brutality with gentleness, we will have the strength of forgiveness and the mind of loving-kindness to overcome those who are brutal and ferocious. In the ancient Indian state of Varanasi, there was a tolerant recluse whom King Kasyapa suspected of being impious. Because of the king's suspicion, the recluse's limbs, nose and ears were amputated. However, at the moment when the order was carried out, the recluse vowed to first teach and transform the king as soon as he reached enlightenment. The king was so moved by the recluse's loving-kindness and compassion that he repented his transgressions and even resolved to support the recluse in his practice. This story shows how loving-kindness is the best remedy for brutality.

2. Compassion can avert malice. If we want to distance ourselves from those who are malicious, or even transform malice into benevolence and beauty, we must have sym-

pathy and compassion. The supernatural beings guarding the Buddha's teachings with their ferocious eyes are actually compassionate and sympathetic in their resolve to restrain and warn demons from doing evil.

In the third century B.C.E., King Asoka of the Maurya Empire converted to Buddhism and found solace in the teachings of the Buddha after he repented all the destruction he had caused in his invasion of Kalinga. By virtue of his transformation from conquest to righteousness, cruelty to compassion, and malice to benevolence, King Asoka taught his people the fundamental principles of morality and service. Because of this change in his temperament, King Asoka left a legacy of kindness and compassion. In addition, the Buddha's chief disciples Sariputra and Purna, well-known for their compassionate sacrifices, put aside their lives for the sake of spreading the Buddha's words in uncivilized lands, for they hoped to transform the lay people's ignorance and correct their errant ways. In short, they too exemplified that compassion is the best remedy for malice and ignorance.

3. Joy can fulfill every good intention. In today's society, some people take pleasure in the misfortune of others and are secretly pleased with the hardship suffered by those they dislike. Moreover, they will also become jealous of another's success. In contrast, people with a joyful mind always take delight in the achievements of either friends or foes. They are always perfectly willing to extend a helping hand to those who are in need of their help. Neither jealous nor envious, they always take pride in the accomplishments of others. Even if they are without fame, fortune, or power, they will not lose their joy. Even if they are impoverished and homeless, they will not allow their hardships to rob them of their happiness. Because they can always maintain joy in their hearts,

they can overcome any difficulty in fulfilling every good intention.

4. Equanimity can assure true liberation. What is equanimity? It is ridding ourselves of attachments and partiality, as well as greed and desire. We should be impartial in offering happiness and hope, and unselfish in our willingness to part with our possessions. If we can control our desire and greed, we will have no trouble gaining true liberation. We will be like Chan Master Jin Bifeng who escaped from the grip of the demon of impermanence by abandoning his attachment to a jade bowl. Therefore, equanimity is the necessary condition for liberation.

The *Flower Adornment Sutra* urges us "to constantly practice the way of forbearance and settle the mind in the states of loving-kindness, compassion, joy, and equanimity." The Four Immeasurables are the basis of our practice and the place for our peaceful abidance, because they are truly sublime in their uses.

One-Word Cues

It is not uncommon for a people to undergo a profound transformation. Their perspective on life can be influenced by the smallest things. Some find a new direction in life just by over-hearing a phrase, while others gain resolve simply by receiving a one-word cue. The following are four of life's one-word cues:

1. "Concession" is a basic virtue of human behavior. As the saying goes, "there are boundless opportunities in taking a step back." From emperors abdicating out of duty to siblings deferring to each other out of familial love, Chinese history is replete with examples of worthy people yielding their positions and advantages. "To make a concession is to show respect, humility, and harmony," says the *Platform Sutra of the Sixth Patriarch*. If every-one could be as modest and humble as possible, there would be less conflict, jealousy, and struggle in the world. People would feel more respected. Xunzi taught, "Whenever there is fighting, there is chaos; whenever there is chaos, there is poverty." To have peace in socie-ty, we must yield willingly and be able to make "conces-sions," a one-word cue to remind us of one of the most important virtues of human conduct.

2. "Righteousness" is the proper way to conduct oneself. In conducting ourselves properly in society, we must abide by the principle of "righteousness" in everything we do. This includes having the right understanding, view, thought, and standpoint. Righteousness is the root of all actions and the foundation of leadership. Confucius said "A person of righteousness will conduct himself proper-ly without being compelled; a person without righteous-

ness will not conduct himself properly even if compelled." If we are righteous and open in our actions, we will not be overcome by hardship or obstacles. Instead, others will follow us willingly on the strength of our conduct and character.

3. "Generosity" is the key to charity. Being generous is the prerequisite for doing good deeds. Contributing time, labor, or money, and giving others a smile or kind word are all acts of goodness. Generosity should be expressed sincerely and without expectation. Nor should it be motivated by the desire to be recognized by others. Otherwise, it will no longer be giving but greed. The practice of giving is genuine when done in accordance with the teachings of the *Diamond Sutra*, where "the giver, the receiver, and what is given are all empty, without exception." It is like the sun shining indiscriminately on earth and the sweet rain nourishing the crops unconditionally. True acts of generosity are without any regret, expectation of return, and thought of personal benefit.

4. "Simplicity" is the essence of true friendship. "The road is long and arduous unless it is traveled in the company of good friends," said Shakespeare, because friends are the most important companions in our life's journey. However, a true friendship must transcend the realm of personal interests and endure the test of life-and-death. Ouyang Xiu, a well-known scholar of the Song Dynasty, noted, "A virtuous man will only befriend those who share his morality, while a petty character will only befriend those who benefit him." If friendships are built on the sands of gain and loss, they will inevitably fall apart when there is a conflict of interest or a loss of prof-

it. Therefore, friends should not be made on the basis of
passion or desire, but on the principles of ethics and propriety instead. It is through the practice of "simplicity"
that friendship can last over time.

While wealth can be exhausted during one's lifetime, truth
is inexhaustible and everlasting. A true teaching is invaluable
when it is beneficial and practical even if it only consists of one
phrase or a one-word cue. Therefore, one-word cues can provide
profound guidance for conducting ourselves in life.

The Four Considerations

Descartes's "I think, therefore, I am" suggests that thought is the driving force behind action, and that without the mind, nothing is possible. Indeed, a person's actions are often the result of thoughtful consideration. If a person considers decisions carefully and correctly, their behavior will bring good results; otherwise, he or she will deviate and have nothing but trouble. Therefore, it is necessary for us to think before we act, and be careful of what we see, hear, say, or do. We should always be mindful of the following four considerations:

1. Given our eyes like to see, we must consider the propriety of the object. In order to enjoy the beautiful and colorful world, we do need to use our eyes. However, before looking at anything, we must discern what we should or should not see, lest our eyes be blinded by certain alluring pleasures of this multi-colored world. As the Confucian saying goes, "Do not look upon impropriety." We must turn our eyes from what is inappropriate or meaningless, especially in a society where law and order are often ignored. For example, we might get a knife in the chest or a punch in the face for casting the wrong glance or being in the wrong place. Therefore, the best way for us to avoid dangerous situations is to consider the propriety of what we see.

2. Given our ears like to listen, we must consider the truthfulness of the sound. "The true essence of the Buddha's teachings is in the purity of its sound." Sentient beings in this *Saha* world have the sharpest hearing faculties. Since our ears are bombarded with information from all directions every day, what we hear can become a source

of unwanted worries if we listen to what should not be heard. Therefore, it is important for our ears to be very deliberate in filtering out lies and rumors. We should "not listen to impropriety." If we do hear anything that is unreasonable or wrong, we should be able to realize it as simply hearsay or gossip.

3. Given our mouth likes to speak, we must consider the appropriateness of our words. Of our eyes, ears, nose and mouth, only the latter has one opening, which suggests we should listen more and speak less. Even if we have something to say, we must be very careful of its consequence, because once it is uttered, there is no way to retrieve it. We should "speak no impropriety." Therefore, it is imperative for us to be circumspect with our words, because careless talk will bring us unwarranted trouble. While we can often speak endlessly on various matters, we should not utter a word when it is inappropriate. Thus, we must consider carefully what we say.

4. Given that matters need to be settled, we must consider the implications of our actions. Before making a decision, we must be rational in our thinking and mindful of the consequences. If a matter benefits other people, we should do our best to carry it out even if we are ridiculed or laughed at. On the other hand, if a matter is detrimental to another's well-being, we must not do it regardless of how many excuses there may be for doing it. Sometimes, people make decisions based on their emotions and moods, and this often results in disastrous consequences for everyone involved. Therefore, before making a decision, we must first consider the consequences—its advantages, disadvantages, benefits, and harm.

Because humans are rational, thinking beings, their innate wisdom can be cultivated and developed. Hence, the Buddhist scriptures teach, "One enters samadhi or perfect concentration through hearing, contemplating, and practicing the Buddha's teachings." Since enlightenment is attained at the highest stage of contemplation, we should be ever mindful of the above considerations.

Four Ways of Cultivation

According to the *Records on Self-Reflection*, "The truly wise harmoniously get along with people, treat subordinates with tolerance and everyone with forgiveness." People must cultivate the virtue of tolerance and forgiveness. Forgiving the unintentional mistakes of others and allowing them the opportunity to change and improve are the practice of the wise. The following are four ways of cultivation:

1. Do not expose the deceit of others. When we discover that our friends have ulterior motives towards us, it is best not to expose them as long as we know what is going on. A Qing scholar asserted, "Respect can calm the anger of another so conflicts can cease." Instead of blaming, scolding, and fighting with others, we should show them we are not vying for power, act humbly and ethically, and treat them with sincerity. We can thus move them into changing their errant ways.

2. Do not be provoked by the insult of others. When others say things that harm or insult us, we should not show any displeasure. If we show our anger with our facial expressions, they will see that we lack cultivation. The Song dynasty scholar Su Dongpo said, "The courageous of the world have no fear of sudden changes and do not get angry with unreasonable demands. Hence, they are capable of major undertakings, and their resolve is far and deep." A person who can tolerate insults from others is truly courageous. Many famous generals in Chinese history became what they were by tolerating insults that were very difficult to bear.

3. Do not publicize the faults of others. Chinese people traditionally practice the virtue of covering up the negativities and communicating the benevolence of others. They generally do not discuss the shortcomings and faults of other people. However, when we encounter criminals, we must comply with the law so that justice is served and the public will not be harmed. In the case of the minor personal mistakes of others or inappropriate speech and behavior, we can give advice and request them to change their ways. We should not casually disclose what we know. By publicizing acts of kindness as much as possible, we provide people the opportunity to learn from the examples of the wise and virtuous, and eradicate unwholesome behavior. As a result, the number of kind deeds in society will increase, and social ethics will improve.

4. Do not be attached to our own kindness we grant others. The ancients said, "Do not forget the kindness we receive from others; do not remember the kindness we give to others." We may have the opportunity to provide others with assistance, contribute some service, or give them some benefit. Yet, we should not be attached to what we do and keep thinking about it. Moreover, we should not expect a payback from people. Buddhism teaches "giving without attachment to form." Even the Bible says, "What the left hand gives should not be told to the right hand." These quotations only illustrate that in giving to others, we should not keep dwelling on our generosity. The Liang Dynasty Emperor Wu built many temples and supported many monastics in his life. However, when he flaunted his deeds to the First Patriarch of Chan, Bodhidharma, responded, "No merit whatsoever." Therefore, giving should not be based on our yearning

for fame, profit, or reward. Giving without any attachment to form is actually the most meritorious.

According to the saying, "Large ambition with a small
capacity cannot achieve any success." The scale of success is in
direct proportion to a person's capacity and magnanimity. When
we have attained these four ways of cultivation in life, we can gain
a mature, realistic, open, and tolerant personality. We will be offering the world loving-kindness and benevolence.

Flexibility in Application

We need to live with a sense of value and purpose so that our life can be useful. To do so, we have to actively rely on all our connections, conditions, and abilities to motivate ourselves so that all of our life force can be brought into full play, and we can be useful.

1. We have to embrace both the ideal and the practical in our daily life. No one can fully neglect the practical aspects of living, since life inevitably presents us with various problems involving people, money, and emotions. In dealing with problems, it is very important for us to harmonize ideals and practice, as well as thoughts and emotions. Some people only focus on mundane matters and not reasoning. Others only pay attention to reasoning and ignore human feelings. Neither type conducts itself according to the Middle Way. In conducting ourselves and dealing with matters, we need to take good care of both the ideal and the practical in order to make life complete.

2. We have to apply what we have learned intelligently. Life is actually a book which we cannot finish studying even in a lifetime. Therefore, we have to learn for as long as we live, and we should apply what we learn intelligently. It is impossible for anyone to remain unchanged or to be totally inflexible. As long as it is beneficial to others, we should do or speak whatever is necessary. Therefore, a truly capable person is resourceful in making use of various conditions to help others and accomplish their goals. They would not mind even if they are wronged or suffer some disadvantage.

3. We have to spread joy among people. We know that no one is an island in the world, and we have to interact with people and their activities all the time. When we are in a community, it is most important to give others joy, sharing with them all things positive. We cannot keep a long face daily or contaminate others with our sorrow and suffering. Nobody will like us, and they will leave us eventually. In today's society, it is not enough to have sound, action, and color. The key is joy. So spreading joy to others is crucial.

4. We have to seek progress in the course of uncertainty. Success has always been the result of trials and experiments. If we are too conservative, fail to keep up with the times, refuse to accept new knowledge, and dare not take up any challenges, we are destined to fall behind the changing times. Therefore, we need to keep innovating, renewing ourselves, and endlessly seeking growth in order to progress in life. Sticking to the old rules and treading on the same spot all the time, we will inevitably find that we have gone nowhere.

If water in a pool is stagnant, it will smell and grow stale, so that it is unsuitable for drinking or washing. If our thinking becomes sluggish and cannot be applied resourcefully, the value of our life will be limited. Thus, we have to pay attention to the above in order to be flexible in the face of life's challenges.

Learning with Diligence

　　Society nowadays advocates lifelong learning. Learning is indeed an endeavor for life, as well as a deeply personal pursuit. Besides our parents, schools, and society that provide us with models, wisdom, and an environment for learning, true learning must come from ourselves. If we do not work hard and pay enough attention, then even with the best teachers and experts on hand, we still cannot learn. Hence, we need to learn diligently with the following guidelines in mind:

1. Eyes must see, and the mouth must speak. When learning, we must watch carefully what our teachers are doing and read the relevant books with similar attention, in order to gain a deeper understanding. Moreover, we should try to emulate the spirit of "reading ten thousand volumes and traveling ten thousand miles" as a student. When traveling to learn, our eyes should be even more alert. We should read the history, geography, customs, and culture of the different regions we visit so as to make our journey worthwhile.

   However, sometimes we may not be able to understand things just by looking. We need to ask questions as well. In Chinese, the term for "learning" is literally "learn and ask." If we do not ask about what we do not understand, we will be unable to learn. Therefore, we should not be shy about asking questions if we truly want to progress.

2. The mind must focus, and the ears must listen. The mind is our master. No matter what we are learning, our mind must remain focused and diligent. If we are not paying full attention, then regardless of how useful the knowl-

edge were are being given, it will not enter our mind and be appreciated. Therefore, we must keep our mind focused and pay attention.

Moreover, we also have to listen well with our ears. Our sense of hearing is a crucial instrument in learning. Buddhist scriptures declare, "This teaching of the truth is pure listening." The keenest sense for sentient beings of the *Saha* world is that of hearing. When we are in the dark or even separated by a wall, we can still hear what others are saying. Therefore, we should make good use of our ears, while cultivating the practice of "listen, contemplate, and practice."

3. The hands must write, and the feet must walk. In learning, we need to analyze, classify, and interpret by taking notes. After reading a book, it is best to write a report on it, or afterwards we should at least write down some quotations, notes, and insights for review. When we listen to lectures, we should also take notes, because as we keep reviewing and studying what we have learned, it will become a part of us. Modern people like to use tape recorders or save information onto their computers, but everything will only become dead data if it is not utilized. Therefore, we need to write with our hands and also walk with our feet. We have to go to libraries to look up any subject we do not know or travel to learn from special teachers. The right attitude is being willing to travel a thousand miles for the sake of learning.

4. The will must be strong, and thinking must be clear. A firm resolve or will is of prime importance in learning. We must have determination and perseverance. When we can work as hard as enduring "ten years toiling in solitude under the cold window," like the paragons of

old, we will be able to achieve "success for the whole world to recognize." We must therefore be diligent in application and persistent in our pursuit, as we explore, research, and analyze the knowledge we gain.

Furthermore, our every thought must be clear. When we speak about cultivation in Buddhism, clear thinking is greatly emphasized. For instance, in reciting Amitabha Buddha's name or doing Chan meditation, every thought must be distinct and clear. When our thinking is clear, it is like seeing fish in clear water. As such, we will have no worries about enhancing our wisdom or success in our learning.

We must know the proper ways to pursue learning. When we pay attention and learn with diligence, we will gain success much more easily.

Leisure and Recreation

After the fields have been farmed for some time, they must be left to fallow. Troops deployed in action for a certain period must be given a break to unwind and recharge themselves. Modern people are paying more attention to leisure and recreation. Their intent is not to make an escape from a busy work schedule, but to enable for more joy and pleasure in life, so that our bodies and minds can relax and gain peace. Thus, we can renew ourselves for a fresh start.

Buddhism also emphasizes "rest," because it enables us to recharge our batteries and, which can then serve as a prerequisite for diligence. However, what is the best recreation that will not waste time, money, and energy? What can we do so that we can truly become revitalized? The following four types of recreation will serve as guidelines:

1. Physical recreation. Do you feel weak and inadequate physically? There are many forms of physical exercise available such as walking, jogging, aerobics, swimming, hiking, or rock climbing. These are ways we can train and improve our physique. Besides strengthening our body, they can also enhance our mental and spiritual being, change our character, improve our confidence, build endurance, and cultivate the courage to overcome difficulties.

2. Adult educational recreation. Lifelong learning has become an important lesson in modern society that has caught the attention of many people. By engaging in learning as recreation, we can satisfy our desire for "further education." Adult educational recreation includes joining study groups, writing, traveling, listening to lec-

tures and seminars, or taking experimental courses. We can learn something new and improve our knowledge while engaging in recreational activities. They can broaden our vision and open our minds.

3. Arts recreation. There are people who enjoy dancing, painting, sculpture, music, singing, drama, or art. By joining organizations and groups in these pursuits, we can entertain ourselves as well as others. Moreover, we can learn from one another by sharing and improving our skills alongside people with similar interests so we can make friends at the same time. Like Wang Po wrote in his famous verse *Preface to Teng Wang Ge*, "A hundred days of recreation, wonderful friends as numerous as clouds."

4. Service recreation. This includes working as volunteers in schools, hospitals, nursing homes, charitable organizations, and foundations, as well as temples and churches. We can help clean the environment, chaperon school children, and care for the sick in hospices. By engaging in service recreation, we can make broad connections with people, enhance our compassion, accumulate experiences, and develop our potential and wisdom. Life will be so more meaningful as we can bring our life force into full play and learn to cherish its value.

Within Buddhist practice, diligence means we should rest and work at the right times. Recreation allows us to relax our busy minds, improve the quality of life, and pursue higher and better productivity. Therefore, we should participate in the right kinds of recreation as indicated above, for these will certainly benefit both our body and mind.

The Middle Way

    In everyday life, some people are over-indulgent in their material pursuits, while others may be too austere with their lifestyle. There are spendthrifts as well as the extremely frugal. Neither extreme represents a natural approach to life. It is like our hands–neither making a fist or stretching our hand all the time is normal. We need to flex and close our hands throughout the day, so as not to keep them in one fixed position. Likewise, every matter in life should be conducted appropriately without going to either extreme. This is the path of the Middle Way. The following are some guidelines on practicing the Middle Way in our daily life:

1. We should not over-exert ourselves at work. We cannot go about life without work, and naturally, we must be diligent in what we do. However, we should not over-exert ourselves too much either; otherwise work will seem more bitter and painful as we slowly burn ourselves out. Therefore, most companies and large corporations these days establish eight-hour workdays for their employees, usually from eight or nine in the morning till around five in the afternoon. In addition, weekends are mostly days off from work. Their purpose is to ensure that employees do not become burned out from their work.

2. We should not be too indulgent with our pleasures. We cannot avoid a material life completely, because proper a dose of materialism is necessary for sustaining life. However, there are people who over-indulge in sensual pleasures. For instance, they only eat gourmet food, wear designer-brand clothing, live in palatial estates, and commute in luxury vehicles. In their pursuit of material

pleasures, they often become wasteful. Like overdrawing on a bank account, they will likely end up heavily in debt. Hence, we should apply moderation in enjoying the fruit of our merits and good fortune.

3. We should not be too harsh towards others. In getting along with others, we need to appreciate the Middle Way. It is crucial that we treat people with magnanimity and consideration. As supervisors, we should especially treat others as we would want ourselves to be treat. In fact, we should be lenient with people and strict with ourselves. Treating others either too harshly or too leniently is not the right approach.

4. We should not be too vain with what we use. Some people simply love to shop. They go shopping even when they have nothing they need and never tire of it. They favor the most fashionable or expensive products over things that are practical and sufficient. In reality, we do not need any luxury products, because too much materialism is not in our best interest for we will end up being enslaved by such objects. Furthermore, an abundance of material possessions can in fact become a burden.

The Middle Way is the Buddha's teaching on avoiding extremes. Being in the middle is not straying off to either extreme. We should be mindful of the above and keep to the Middle Way.

The Benefits of Cultivation

A house needs repair from time to time and our clothes require mending when they are torn. The deeds committed by our ears, eyes, nose, tongue, and body often err. If we do not rectify our mistakes, it would be like not fixing broken objects that only end up in the garbage. Therefore, cultivating our body and mind should be the top priority in life. The following are some benefits of cultivation:

1. Cultivation ensures elegance. We need to pay attention to how we walk, stand, sit, and sleep. Buddhism teaches us to "walk like the wind, stand like a pine, sit like a bell, and sleep like a bow." To assure that our every word and action is appropriate, we need to truly infuse the kindness and benevolence within us into our root organs of eyes, ears, nose, tongue, and body, for only then will we demonstrate elegant poise and gain the respect of others. Some people believe that having money is everything, so they pay no attention to their conduct. While money can buy new clothes, the person wearing them may not appear so graceful. Money can also buy cosmetics, but putting them on does not necessarily result in elegance.

   Our poise relies on cultivation at all times and is nurtured from within, not from some makeover on the outside. Some people may not have the best looking features, but when they have an elegant poise that comes from cultivation, they are just as attractive. Therefore, we can easily detect a person's cultivation from his or her facial expressions and conduct.

2. Cultivation ensures a dignified demeanor. People will

not take us seriously when our body language is uncouth and exaggerated, nor will they tolerate us when we jump and prance about all the time. It is important to be dignified and poised according to circumstances. We should not stand when we should sit, and vice versa. When we speak, our facial expression and bodily gestures should also be in accordance with the right etiquette. When our demeanor and expressions are proper, we will naturally gain people's respect. Some people lose their poise on hearing a negative phrase or act rudely when faced with an obstacle. They are clearly short on cultivation.

3. Cultivation ensures kind speech and action. No matter how high a position we hold, how great our power is, or how much money we own, if our speech and actions are arrogant and rude, no one will respect us. The Buddha's Light International Association advocates, "Do good deeds, speak kind words, and have positive thoughts." This means that what we say or do should be pleasing to others. We should not be wordy or banal in our speech. We must pay attention to any words that may harm others and any action that is rude and improper. Our speech and actions should inspire the strength of fellowship, so that others will like to be with us. If talking to us is like basking in a warm sun and if watching us is like watching art in motion, then people will naturally come from near and far to be friends with us.

4. Cultivation ensures proper movements. Confucius said, "Do not look upon, listen to, speak of, or perform any impropriety." If we are serious about our own cultivation, we should speak and act accordingly. We need to know how and when to move forward or take a step back. Nowadays, people often speak loudly at the wrong

time and keep quiet when they should speak up. The *Discourses of the Buddha* actually point out that one of the five kinds of inhumanity is "not speaking when one should." Yet, if a person often speaks nonsense or is long-winded in speech, even their family will become annoyed. If we have no idea where we should stand or sit, then even though heaven and earth may be large, there is still no place for us. Hence, people who are serious about cultivation know how and when to advance and retreat when visiting friends, doing their job, relating to family members, or attending social functions.

Cultivating our body and mind is of prime importance in life and has many benefits of which we need to be mindful.

Four Gains

What people wish for and seek in their lives varies. They may wish for money, material possessions, fame, fortune, love, human connections, or trust. But how do we properly gain what we seek? The following are some approaches to gaining some things in life:

1. Reading allows us to gain knowledge. The ancients said, "One is never too old to learn." We cannot possibly learn all the knowledge in the world in one lifetime. Therefore, we must read everyday in order to gain more knowledge. Reading allows us to understand the truth and prepare for the future. Books are sources of wisdom, the catalyst behind human progress, literary treasures for knowing the past and making sense of the present, and vehicles for understanding the standards of behavior in dealing with people and situations. We can enhance our abilities through books, because they give us knowledge.

2. Work allows us to gain experience. In order to succeed, we must not be afraid of difficulties or failure. Dr. Sun Yat-sen's career as a revolutionary met with no success during the first ten tries. It was only with the eleventh try that he was able to overthrow the decaying dynasty. If we have perseverance in everything we do, we can gain much experience through work. Experiences can be obtained through either failure or success. In failure, we can gain from introspection and improvement, while in success, we can gain from better planning and organization. Therefore, whether it is through success or failure, we can always gain precious experience and skill as long as we work hard.

3. Human connections allow us to gain expediency. When
we develop human connections, we gain good relationships with people. There are people who meet obstacles
at every step of the way, whereas others find smooth sailing everywhere they go. They are welcomed by everyone they come across. The difference lies in making
connections. In our everyday life, a warm smile, a word
of praise, a simple act of service, or sincere caring
expression for others can bring people much joy, thus
promoting harmony in human relationships. It is also the
beginning of making a connection with others. When we
have positive connections, we are actually gaining expediency and ease in whatever we do. With good human
relationships, we will be able to complete our goals
much more easily.

4. The Dharma allows us to gain joy. When the Buddha
spoke the Dharma, his intention was to explain its meaning so as to bring us happiness. In other words, the purpose of the Buddha's teachings is to give sentient beings
joy. Because the world is filled with suffering due to old
age, sickness, death, inequalities between classes, and the
conflicts between self and others, the Buddha sought
solutions for sentient beings to get rid of suffering and
gain joy. He first traced the roots of our suffering to our
greed, anger, and delusion, and then taught us the way to
eliminate them so that we could realize to our true
nature. Through the guidance of his teaching, we can
find direction for settling our mind and life, and gain joy
through the Dharma.

We should start reading at a young age, and we should also
learn how to read people, events, and our physical environment.
Even more importantly, we must know how to get along well with
people because this will benefit us in our work and career. In real-

ity, studying and working are both necessary for living a stable and peaceful life. However, it takes cultivation and realization of the Dharma to raise our spirituality to higher levels.

Four Comforts

People generally look to fulfill their wishes hoping that everything will go well in their life. For instance, they wish for increases in their bank accounts, spiritual contentment, praise, and approval from others. These are some of the comforts in life. However, external matters are unreliable because once causes and conditions change, circumstance will change at the same time. We can only create a comfortable life through our own effort. The following are some guidelines to creating a truly comfortable life:

1. Having no preoccupations is precious. The ancients explained, "Everything can be forgotten; those who can, imbibe three cups of wine; those who cannot, dwell on the fading glory." We all seek fortune, status, honor, and the respect of others. But if "being comfortable in life is supreme, then why would anyone yearn for high positions thousands of miles away?" asks a Six Dynasties text. When a tree is large, it catches wind; when one's reputation is great, it attracts jealousy. Various kinds of slander, setbacks, troubles, and stress can come on the heels of fame and fortune, while having an ordinary mind without a care in the world is truly precious. When we do not have any preoccupations, we will not be deluded by the obscuring "dust" of the world. Without worries on our mind, we can find peace everywhere we go, and our life will become carefree.

2. Knowing contentment is wealth. The Hakka people have a beautiful saying, "I am content" meaning "I'm satisfied; I've had enough." Is there anything more enriching than having such an attitude in life? If we are looking to make a lot of money, we must realize that money and afflic-

tions are brothers. Once we have money, we cannot escape from constant afflictions. In seeking fame, we also need to understand that attachment and fame are one and the same. When fame does arrive, we will inevitably be worried about losing it. Therefore, being content is true wealth.

The *Bequeathed Teachings of the Buddha* says, "People who are content may sleep on the floor yet still be at ease; people not appreciating contentment may live in heaven yet still be unhappy." People who are discontent are bound by desires while those who appreciate simplicity consider rising above material desires as their wealth.

3. Walking in peace is transportation. As technology advances, our means of transportation improves, and with it, people's cravings also increase. People have gone from using bicycles to motorcycles and eventually cars as their mode of transportation. When domestic models were no longer satisfactory, they looked for imported models because they were more distinctive looking. Nowadays, the rich may even be dissatisfied with a luxury car as they vie for a helicopter or an airplane.

Even when we have everything we want, our hearts are still not at peace. We are unhappy because we fear our vehicles may be stolen, broken into, towed away, or destroyed in a crash. There is always the concern over finding a parking space or being vandalized. In reality, we should not be seeking sensual pleasures in life. We should walk more often, instead of always driving or being chauffeured. When we are happy with a simple life practicing the Way, we will have more leisure and fewer hassles dealing with traffic. Our health will also improve as we exercise more.

4. Eating in moderation is nourishment. During the Warring States Period, the King of Qi tried to recruit Yan Chu to become an official in his imperial court by offering him many luxurious privileges and material benefits. However, Yan turned everything down saying he did not need any fame or fortune, nor any gourmet meals. All he wanted was to be an ordinary citizen, eating only when he was hungry because then any food would be more appetizing. The Tang scholar Zhang Baoyun also explained, "At a sumptuous feast, what is consumed only satiates the mouth." In Buddhist monasteries, eating a meal is called "passing the hall," meaning eating is solely for nourishing the physical body. Thus, we are just passing through and not attached to the food itself. If we can truly appreciate the taste of simplicity, we can sustain ourselves over the long run.

We need to dress according to the changing weather and adjust our body and mind with changes in the environment. No matter what we are doing in life, we must act appropriately. Men and women should marry someone of a compatible age, our shoes must be of a comfortable size, and food must be properly seasoned. In dealing with situations, we need to react appropriately, either advancing or retreating. When we come across chances to learn or do business, we should appreciate such opportunities. Furthermore, we should do our best at our jobs so we will not be afraid of falling behind the times. In getting along with others, we need to exercise restraint because if we only do what pleases us while infringing on others, our relationships with them will certainly be jeopardized. Clearly, these reminders concerning the four comforts in life can benefit all of us.

The Fragrance of Flowers

The world needs the fragrance of flowers. Everyone loves flowers because as they bloom with a myriad colors and produce fragrance, the world becomes so much more delightful. This is why people who are good-looking or ethical are sometimes compared to flowers. Not only do flowers enrich our lives, but they also allow us to express our thoughts and beautify our intentions.

Flowers are closely related to our existence, because they play an important role in improving the quality of our daily life. For instance, in any celebration or party, a floral arrangement can fill the room with fragrance and beauty. In expressing our good wishes for celebrating birthdays, welcoming guests, or visiting the sick, a bouquet of flowers helps us convey love and affection. Indeed, the world relies heavily on the fragrance of flowers. The following are some views on the value of flowers:

1. Flowers adorn our mundane world. Flowers are the essence of nature's living beauty, as well as the best decoration for our home and the most wonderful adornment in life. "The moon is ordinary outside the window; but the plum blossoms in the foreground make it all entirely different." With their delicate charm, fragrance, and purity, flowers enrich nature and our spiritual life, adding many colors to our common world as they spread their charm with splendor.

2. Flowers enhance the brightness of life. From the Buddhist perspective, the lifespan of flowers as they bloom and wither is the best symbol of life. When a flower blossoms, it is like the birth of a new life, reminding us to appreciate the value of life. Once the flower withers, we can also realize the emptiness and imperma-

nence of life, prompting us to make the best use of the here and now. Within a lifespan, how do we bloom with passion like a flower? How do we live life to the fullest by sprinkling splendor and glory onto the world? That is the spirit we must learn from flowers.

3. Flowers represent the diversity of life. Flowers are the beautiful ambassadors of art. The kaleidoscope of flowers in all their shapes and colors reflect a variety of characteristics that make them fitting metaphors for the lasting image of one's existence. Different flowers, as well as shrubs and plants, have often be used as metaphors for different kinds of lives. The Song Dynasty scholar Zhou Dunyi, in his "Love of Lotus," wonderfully integrated the characteristics and styles of both flowers and people to express his spirit. He wrote, "Tao Yuanming loved chrysanthemums¡Kworldly people love peonies¡Kwhile I only love the purity of lotuses as they grow out of mud without being defiled¡K" He also noted similes such as, "Tao Yuanming was a hermit like the chrysanthemum," and "although worldly people love wealth like the peony, I prefer to be a gentleman like the lotus." Therefore, flowers can also be symbols of the different styles of life.

4. Flowers express the true meaning of human sentiments. We all love flowers because in addition to their being objects of appreciation, they can also express love and friendship. The various expressions and intentions flowers convey enhance the sharing of sentiments and feelings between self and others. For example, roses mean love, lilies friendship, carnations motherly love, peonies wealth, and orchids elegance and purity. Hence, people use flowers to show their will, express love and admiration, and convey sorrow. Flowers are also given to con-

gratulate a person's achievements and as symbols of blessings. Buddhism often uses flowers as metaphors too. There is even a Buddhist scripture called *The Lotus Sutra of Wondrous Dharma*, which compares the profound Dharma to a beautiful lotus. The world benefits from the fragrance of flowers as it does from the Dharma.

Flowers and Buddhism have a very deep connection. The purity, gentleness, and beauty of flowers best symbolize a heart full of respect and devotion. Buddhists make offerings of flowers to the Buddha. A petal offered in the ten directions can represent endless sincerity. Besides symbolizing the purity of Buddhas and bodhisattvas, flowers also act as a form of communication for devotees. As Buddhism teaches, "While the *Saha* world in which we live is full of defilements, we must persist in being a pure lotus."

The Way to a Bountiful Harvest

We all look for a bountiful harvest in life. For instance, farmers want a bumper crop, investors a good return on their capital, and students higher grades. If we wish for good results, we must first make the sacrifices and do the work hard. The following are four keys to a bountiful harvest:

1. If we want a bumper crop, we must till the land. If we want a good harvest, we must plow in the spring and cultivate in the summer, so that we may have enough grain to store in the autumn. In this way, we will not have to worry about the severe winter. Likewise, writers till their creation on paper as they burn the midnight oil, devoting their life to their art. Teachers patiently write on the blackboard, guiding their students in a tireless effort so as to establish their character and intellect. Chan practitioners cultivate their mind-field with every successive thought, as they seek to break through delusion and settle their body and mind.

2. If we want good fortune, we must be generous in giving. Good fortune allows us to live in comfort, and it is something we all want. However, we must first plant the seed of giving if we are seeking good fortune. "Such is the cause; such is the effect." If we do not give, others will not give to us either. Without contributing anything, it is difficult for us to gain anything. Therefore, giving is planting seeds, and with the seed of giving, we will enjoy the fruit of wealth.

3. If we wish for longevity, we must be compassionate.

Most people like to pray to gods and deities for prosperity, a long life, and happiness. The truth is that gods, bodhisattvas, and Buddhas do not give us good fortune or a long life. It is only ourselves who can do so. If we give people joy, respect their rights, and assist them accordingly, we can naturally live a long life. Human life is not just the number of years our physical body can live. It is the lengthening of our life of wisdom. "In seeking fortune, one should seek lasting fortune; in wishing for longevity, one should wish for the infinite life of wisdom." Moreover, our life does not only reside in our body, but lives in our words, virtues, and career. When we can leave our mark on history, compassion to society, and beauty in the world, we will be living much longer lives.

4. If we want wisdom, we must cultivate *prajna*. Intelligence and wisdom are not bestowed by heaven, nor do they materialize out of thin air. If we want wisdom, we must cultivate *prajna*. *Prajna* is our innate nature, our true face, and the origin of all wisdom. Cultivating *prajna* is the cultivation of our mind. When our mind is clear, then everything can be understood. *Prajna* is thus the treasury of life.

Ultimately, we should not only look for a bountiful harvest in the material world outside of ourselves, but we must also cultivate our spiritual or inner world. The latter is the way to attain a true harvest that can last over time.

Keys to a Long Life

People today put much emphasis on "cultivating life" in order to achieve health and longevity. Because of an abundance of material resources, life has become very comfortable for many people, but we also need good health in order to enjoy life. We can all try to stay healthy through the following ways:

1. Wake and sleep appropriately. The ancients "worked at sunrise and rested at sunset." They kept a regular schedule in their daily life. So even though medical science was not well developed then, people did not get sick easily. In today's world, many people burn the midnight oil working through the night, maintaining an inverted schedule. As a result, there are many more modern-day sicknesses that were unheard of previously. This only illustrates the importance for starting and finishing the day properly. When we keep a routine schedule in tune with our circadian rhythm and live our days accordingly, we are on the first step of maintaining good health.

2. Eat moderately. Many illnesses of modern people are the result of an improper diet. The most common is overeating resulting in obesity. In the past, our elders often reminded us to eat more in order to live a long life. Nowadays, doctors are telling us we should eat less to stay healthy. We should eat three daily meals at the proper time and in the right amount. We should never indulge in eating binges. According to most recommendations, we should "eat a good breakfast, have a full lunch, and only consume a light dinner." When we eat in moderation, we can stay healthy.

3. Work reasonably. Work is the prerequisite for our survival. It is the source of income as well as an important part of our mental well-being, because our work brings value to life. Therefore, we all need to work. However, if we keep overworking for a long period of time, it will take a heavy toll on us and can actually become the invisible assassin of our health. So when we work appropriately, we can live a healthy long life.

4. Exercise regularly. Proper exercising is also an indispensable requirement for good health. We can jog, play ball, swim, walk, bike, lift weights, or work out in the gym everyday. These are all simple regimens that anyone can practice and maintain on a regular basis.

5. Keep a joyful heart. Our body and mind affect each other. When we are sick, our mind will also suffer as there seems to be no joy in life. Likewise, if we are distressed and unhappy, our mental state also affects our physical health negatively. Therefore, keeping a joyful heart at all times is a basic condition for a long life.

6. Do not fight with the world. In life, we of course need to give our best effort in what we do. However, we must bear in mind that we should not dwell on petty contests, constantly bickering with others over fame, power, and profit. "Without fighting, there will be peace and harmony." When we are not fighting with others, we can naturally maintain good health and harmony.

7. Do not crave material possessions. If we excessively crave gratification in the course of enjoying material pleasures, we will often end up their slave. Hence, if we

do not crave material possessions, our body and mind will be at ease.

8. Live in simplicity and peace. Very often in life, when things are meant to be ours, they will come to us without our asking. For things that we should not have, we will not get them even if we try very hard. Therefore, people who appreciate the Buddha's law of dependent origination will follow causes and conditions in every matter. In facing life, whether it is about gain or loss, right or wrong, good or bad, having or not having, such people will take it in stride without attachment and face every situation with a calm mind. This is the best way to nourish a long healthy life.

If we want to live in good health and enjoy longevity, we need to be aware of the above suggestions.

Global Citizens

People should expand their vision of the world. Nowadays, people should think of the world they live in as a global village. We should all be global citizens who live in peace, working together as a team and showing respect and tolerance for one another.

2003 was the fiftieth anniversary of my Dharma teaching career in Taiwan. I have spent two-thirds of my life there. If I am not Taiwanese, then what am I? While no one in Taiwan would recognize me as being culturally Taiwanese, if I go back to mainland China, the people there will still call me a monk from Taiwan. In short, no matter where I go, I am not considered a local. Therefore, I console myself by saying, "I am a global citizen." In retrospect, I do not want to be a citizen of any particular region. As long as the good earth is not rejecting me, I can be a global citizen. So, how do we conduct ourselves as a global citizen? The following are some guidelines:

1. Open our eyes and admire the world. When we look around at the world, we can see that the world is a large place with its myriad vistas and sights that vie in beauty. Mountains, rivers, and forests compete for our attention. Many living beings are there ready to display their beauty. As a global citizen, we must open our eyes wide and thoroughly admire the many noble and beautiful people, deeds, and places the world offers us.

2. Be sure-footed and travel the world. As a global citizen, we should not confine ourselves to small circles. From our travels and daily contacts with the world, we will come to understand it better. What we see and hear will no longer just be the abstract knowledge we learn from

books. Instead, we will gain first-hand knowledge from our travel. How large our world can become does not hinge merely on the extent of our travel, but also on the magnanimity of our perspective.

3. Open our arms and embrace the world. Every great person in the past had the universe in his or her heart. According to the Buddhist teachings, "A mind embraces the cosmos; its capacity can hold as many realms as grains of sand." A Chinese saying also asserts, "One can even row a boat in the belly of a lord." Therefore, as a global citizen, we should have a broad mind. When we open our arms to embrace the globe, then everything is ours. Everything will become very endearing, compelling us to support and nurture it.

4. With the Buddha's light shining, we enjoy the world. The sun shines on every land in the world, and a gentle breeze blows over each corner. It is like the compassion and truth of the Buddha universally and equally providing each sentient being the benefits of the Dharma. Therefore, this world is truly worth our affection and care. Each of us should cherish the sun, the air, the water, the earth in common, and all the produce they provide. With all the beautiful things for us to share, what would be the point of insisting on where one is from, or where one belongs?

Modern means of transportation and telecommunication are very convenient. The entire world is progressing toward globalization, and we are already part of a global village. As its citizens, can we afford not keeping in step with the changing times and become a global citizen?

The Way of Equanimity

Chan Buddhism teaches "The mind of equanimity is the Way!" Yet, some people always speak with the intention to provoke others or handle situations in such as way as to upset heaven and earth. In reality, sometimes it is more intimate to simply talk casually about everyday affairs and more inclusive to just accommodate others. In cultivating the Way, we should focus on what all can practice well–that is, the way of equanimity. When we can experience the truth of the Dharma in everyday matters, it is true cultivation. The following are some definitions of the way of equanimity:

1. Sure and sound words are ordinary speech. We need not speak fancy words or be unconventional in what we say, because the purpose of speech is to communicate clearly with others. We should instead speak firmly and realistically. We should never say empty words or be lofty in expressing ourselves. When we are unrealistic and frivolous in what we say, we will be just "talking the talk but not walking the walk." Worse still, we may offend others with our words, and they will look down on us. Hence, sure and sound words constitute ordinary speech.

2. Keeping to one's role makes a happy person. How should we conduct ourselves? It is imperative that we follow our role and fulfill our duty. For instance, we should be righteous, honest, and compassionate when the situation warrants. As children we should practice filial piety, and as students we should study well and repay the efforts of our teachers with our best effort. If we work for a company or an organization, we should do our job to the best of our ability. When we conduct ourselves

according to our role, we will be a happy person.

3. Evenness in emotions is our true disposition. People have feelings and are, therefore, emotional beings. However, some people are too passionate, but their passion only lasts for five minutes and cannot be sustained. Moreover, their emotions are too complicated and overwhelming, so that others find it difficult to deal with them. Therefore, when relationships are kept simple and feelings even, they can last much longer and will actually be more appealing over time. Hence, evenness in emotions is desirable.

4. A repentant mind is a mind on the right path. Why do people follow a religion? A very important reason is to cultivate humility and awareness of our shortcomings. We should be repentant of our shortcomings towards our parents, children, country, and humanity. With our lack of ability and virtue as well as an insufficient purity of mind, we have to strive even harder in order to make up for these inadequacies.

How should we do so? We can follow the teachings of the Dharma that open up a whole new inner world. People with humility and acceptance of their shortcomings will naturally be diligent in their cultivation.

All phenomena are impermanent, and all forms are empty. If we have a mind of equanimity, then we will approach life with acceptance and openness. We will take life as "flowers in a mirror or the moon in the water," no matter whether we gain or lose. This way our life will be carefree and tranquil.

The Key to Harmony

What is the most important and valuable thing in this world? Peace! What is the most important and valuable thing for people with respect to our fellow humans, society, and nature? Harmony. The following are some keys to peace and harmony:

1. Gentle and beautiful music brings harmony. Music expresses emotions and thoughts. It can shape social trends and mores. Its ability to attract, inspire, and pull at the heartstrings makes it the most beautiful means to affect people. Music has no boundaries, for regardless of its origins or nationality, a piece of beautiful music can mesmerize its listeners. People from different countries may not understand each other's language, but there is always music. Through beautiful rhythms, we can enhance friendship so that harmony among people of different ethnicities and countries can be achieved.

2. Birds chirping in the forests bring serenity. The chirping of birds and twittering of insects are part of nature's support for humanity. When we keep in touch with nature daily, we can temper our personality. For instance, listening to birds twitter in the depth of the woods can be a profound joy in life. It can expand our heart to reach out far and wide, that dissuades us from bickering and fighting over minor matters with others or, worse still, becoming enemies. Communing with nature will help us realize how meaningless it is to bicker over petty matters.

3. The scent of incense and the fragrance of flowers bring

contentment and joy. "An elegant room does not need to be big, and fragrant flowers need not be abundant." Within a neat and tidy room, we can light some fine incense to relax us, providing ease and happiness. We can go walk in the park at our leisure and bask in the perfume of flowers that open our hearts with contentment and joy. Nothing is more appealing in the world than the fragrance of incense and flowers!

4. Stillness without a sound brings tranquility. In the course of a day, we spend time with others, but we also need moments by ourselves that enable us to reside in peace and quiet. During the week, there should also be a few hours for us to be alone in order to calm down. "Tranquility goes a long way." Within the realm of quietude, we can be completely at ease and relaxed.

According to the saying, "Purity and quietness in the ears bring much harmony." A song will only sound good if its music is harmonious. In getting along with people within a community, whenever there is harmony there will be peace, friendliness, joy, congeniality, mutual support, and good fortune. Hence, we need to pay attention to these keys to harmony.

The Key to Live in Peace

If a practitioner can live in peace and contentment, his or her "Way" will naturally flourish. Similarly, people from all walks of life also need to feel settled in their professions before they can find fulfillment. Our body and mind need to live in peace and ease and what follows are some guidelines for doing so:

1. When living in peace and quiet, we still need to be alert to danger. According to one saying, "People without regard for the future, inevitably end up having concerns close at hand." When things are calm, we have to think of how to deal with emergencies and accidents. For instance, even amidst fame and fortune, we should be aware of what should to do if we find ourselves in a dire situation? Even as we prosper in a high position, we should consider how to handle ourselves when impermanence strikes and we have to step down? *The Book of Odes* reminds us, "Before the heavens become dark with rain, I gather bark from the roots of the trees and weave it tightly, in order to make the window and door of my abode." This illustrates the importance of being aware of danger in times of peace and being prepared, so that we will not be troubled when misfortune descends upon us.

2. When living in fortune, we need to think of distant trouble. When we are doing well and everything is going smoothly, we cannot afford to rely on tour fortune and become complacent. Looking at history, numerous rulers were living in affluence and comfort, but because of their ignorance over the possibility of their demise, they lost their kingdom and their lives. In the midst of the most prosperous reign of the Tang Dynasty, Wei

Zheng, the minister renowned for his wisdom, courage, and foresight, counseled Emperor Tai saying, "When in a high and vulnerable position, one needs to think of humility; when blessed with overflowing abundance, one needs to think of loss; when in prosperity, one needs to think of frugality." Likewise, we must remind ourselves frequently even if we are enjoying great fortune because we need to "Be vigilant in life so as to be at peace in death."

3. When living in abundance, we need to relieve the needy. When we are living in wealth and prosperity, we should help in emergencies and support the needy. Some people respond to charity work with the thought, "I should wait until I have more money to give." People like that are miserly in giving and in their lifetime will never find any money to donate, because the day they have extra money to help others will never arrive. Therefore, when we have more money than what we need for our basic needs in life, why wait to help others? Mencius once said, "All people have a heart of mercy." Charity for the needy is therefore the way to cultivate our compassion.

4. When in high position, we need to be mindful of humility. If people in high positions do not care for the hardships of their subordinates and treat the latter with arrogance, an organization's tenuous harmony will be shattered as complaints and grudges grow over time. Therefore, people in high positions must treat their subordinates with sincerity and kindness. Moreover, they have to be prepared for unforeseen changes, because one day they will have to give up their position and plan for a new life.

Sunzi, the famed strategist, said, "The wise think of both gain and loss." People with wisdom will not think of just one side of any matter. They will consider the pros and cons of the whole situation. Even on the verge of triumph, they will make contingency plans for possible failure so that there will be a way out of the situation. This is the way to live in peace for the wise, for after all, "Tasks can be accomplished with preparation but fail without them."

The Way to Peace

The greatest wish for humanity is peace. While most people hope for peace, some opportunists and warmongers have no concern for humanity's harmony and welfare. They prefer to sacrifice human lives in order to promote themselves. However, there needs to be a way for every individual to attain peace. The following are some guidelines:

1. Use selflessness to work for peace. Even though most of humanity advocates world peace these days, we still tend to put the "I" onto a very high pedestal and become attached to our own ego. Everything we do focuses on "I think," "I suppose," or "I believe." The concept of "I" can never lead to peace for anyone. *The Lotus Sutra* points out, "People with too deep a perspective of the self are like hungry ghosts." "I" is the source of conflict while being selfless can achieve justice for all. With justice there will be peace. Hence, if we are looking for world peace, we must first cultivate selflessness as it provides the best foundation for lasting peace.

2. Use compassion to advocate peace. Though we hope for peace, if we treat others with anger and hate, how can there be peace? If we are always greedy and focused on what others can give us, how can we gain peace? We must begin by treating others with compassion by helping them alleviate their suffering. When everyone treats each other with compassion, all sentient beings can enjoy happiness and prosperity, and only then will the world be at peace.

3. Use respect to seek peace. While we all want to be respected by others, we often neglect to give them the

respect they are due. "Do not do to others what you do not want to be done to you" is the basic principle for respect between self and others.

During the Warring States Period, the prime minister and general of the Zhao Kingdom had mutual respect for one another in their show of solidarity. Their unity averted an attack from another kingdom. The five fingers of our hand work in harmony so they can unite to form a fist which has far more strength than any individual finger. We must have solidarity before we can seek peace. Therefore, in the pursuit of lasting peace, we must first establish respect for one another so that it can sustain a lasting peace.

4. Use equality to realize peace. After the Buddha attained enlightenment under the Bodhi tree, he declared, "All sentient beings have the wisdom and merit of a Buddha." This declaration of equality between the Buddha and sentient beings is truly the lamp of liberation for all sentient beings. The Buddha went on to establish the Sangha, the monastic community, on the basis of the "six principles of harmony and respect," in order to assure democracy and equality within the community through its philosophy, laws, finance, language, conduct, and mission. The Buddha always asserted, "I do not rule the community; I am also a member of the Sangha." He lived in the Sangha community on an equal basis with the other monastics, never posing as a ruler. If we want to see a world at peace, we must first call on the people of the world to cultivate a sense of equality for all. Only then can large and small nations with all their races and ethnicities coexist on an equal footing. It is only through a heart of equality that peace can be attained.

In our pursuit of peace, we need to work on these four approaches.

Glossary

Amitabha Buddha: The Buddha of the Western Pure Land, also known as the Buddha of Infinite Light. Amitabha Buddha is described as vowing to purify a realm for those who desire to seek rebirth there by earnestly reciting his name. Sometimes known as Amita Buddha or Amitayus Buddha (the Buddha of Infinite Life.)

Avalokitesvara Bodhisattva: The Bodhisattva of Compassion who can manifest in any conceivable form to bring help to those in need. In China, Avalokitesvara Bodhisattva is usually portrayed in a female form, and also known as the Bodhisattva "Guanyin."

Bodhi: "Awakened" or "enlightened." In the state of *bodhi*, one is awakened to one's own Buddha Nature, having eliminated all afflictions and delusions, and achieved prajna-wisdom.

Bodhisattva: An enlightened being. It is a compound word made up of "*bodhi*" and "*sattva*." *Bodhi* means "enlightened" and *sattva* means "being." Therefore, the term *bodhisattva* refers to a being that has attained enlightenment through practicing all six *paramitas*. Bodhisattvas vow to remain in the world, postponing their own full enlightenment by entering nirvana, in order to liberate all beings. The *bodhisattva* ideal is the defining feature of Mahayana Buddhism.

Buddha: Literally "The awakened one." Used as a generic term to refer to one who has achieved enlightenment and attained complete liberation from the cycle of existence (see *samsara*). More commonly used to refer to the Sakyamuni Buddha, the historical founder of Buddhism (581-501 B.C.E.). He was born the prince of Kapilavastu and the son of King Suddhodana. At the age of twenty-nine, he left the royal palace and his family to search for the meaning of existence. Six years later, he attained enlightenment under the Bodhi tree. He then spent the next forty-five years expounding his teachings, which include the Four Noble Truths, the Noble Eightfold Path, the Law of Cause and Effect, and the Twelve Links of Dependent Origination. At the age of eighty, he entered the state of *parinirvana*.

Buddha Nature: The true nature or inherent potential for achieving Buddhahood that exists in all beings.

Chan: A school of Buddhism that emphasizes enlightenment through deep concentration, meditation, and internal cultivation. Practicing Chan Buddhism does not rely upon intellectual reasoning, analysis of doctrine, or academic studies, but instead, relies upon a profound inner concentration that can reveal and illuminate one's true nature. (The term is pronounced "Zen" in Japanese.)

Dharma: Literally "that which is preserved or maintained." Usually refers to the teachings of the Buddha. When capitalized, it means: 1) the ultimate truth and 2) the teachings of the Buddha. When the Dharma is applied or practiced in life it is referred to as: 3) righteousness or virtue. When it appears with a lowercase "d" it means: 4) anything that can be thought of, experienced, or named; close in meaning to the word "phenomena."

Five Aggregates: Indicating form, feelings, perceptions, mental formation, and consciousness, which together and *interdependently* constitute what we commonly regard as an "individual personality." Also known as the "*five skandhas*."

Five Contemplations for Eating: Five contemplations of which practitioners should be mindful when they take their meals. They include being grateful for the effort in producing and making the food; making sure one's heart and mind is pure and deserving of the offering; guarding oneself against greed in consuming the food; treating the food as medicine to nourish the body; and accepting the food as sustenance on the path of spiritual cultivation.

Five Precepts: Guiding principles in Buddhism that teach proper conduct. These are: 1) no killing, 2) no stealing, 3) no sexual misconduct, 4) no lying, and 5) no taking of intoxicating substances.

Four Elements: In Buddhism, all matters are composed of the elements of earth, water, fire, and wind.

Four Immeasurables: This refers to: 1) the state of boundless loving-kindness in giving others happiness; 2) the state of boundless compassion in liberating others from suffering; 3) the state of boundless joyfulness in keeping others away from suffering; 4) the state of boundless equanimity in treating others equally and without discrimination.

Four Noble Truths: One of the most fundamental Buddhist teachings about the nature and existence of suffering: 1) the truth of suffering, 2) the truth of the cause of suffering, 3) the truth of cessation of suffering, and 4) the truth of the path leading to the cessation of suffering.

Guanyin: Popular Chinese reference to Avalokitesvara Bodhisattva.

Humanistic Buddhism: The primary teaching of the Venerable Master Hsing Yun, which emphasizes putting Buddhism into practice in our daily life, and building a pure land in this human world.

Kalpa: A unit of temporal measurement used in ancient India, that signifies an immense and inconceivable length of time. Buddhism adapted it to refer to the time between the creation and re-creation of worlds.

Karma: Defined as "work, action, or deeds" and is related to the Law of Cause and Effect. All mental, verbal, and physical deeds that are governed by *intention*, both good or bad, produce effects. The effects may be experienced instantly, or they may accumulate and not come into fruition for many years or even many lifetimes.

Law of Cause and Condition: A universal truth in Buddhism based on the dependent origination of all phenomena in primary causes and secondary causes (conditions). The seed out of which a plant or a flower grows is a good illustration of a primary cause. The elements of soil, water, sunlight could be considered the necessary conditions for growth.

Law of Cause and Effect: This is the most basic doctrine in Buddhism, which explains the formation of all relations and connections in the world. This law shows that the arising of each and every phenomenon is due to its own causes and conditions, while the actual form, or manifestation, of all phenomena is the effect.

Mahayana: Literally, "The Great Vehicle," referring to one of the two main traditions of Buddhism, the other being Theravada. Mahayana Buddhism stresses that helping all sentient beings attain enlightenment is more important than just self-liberation.

Nirvana: Literally "extinction," but also can mean "calmed, quieted, tamed, or ceasing." In Buddhism, it refers to the absolute extinction of individual existence, or of all afflictions and desires; it is the state of liberation, beyond birth and death. It is also the final spiritual goal for all branches of Buddhism.

Noble Eightfold Path: Eight right ways leading to the cessation of suffering according to the Four Noble Truths as taught by the Buddha. They are: 1) right view; 2) right thought; 3) right speech; 4) right action; 5) right livelihood; 6) right effort; 7) right mindfulness; and 8) right concentration.

Prajna: Literally "consciousness" or "wisdom." As the highest form of wisdom, *prajna* is the wisdom of insight into "emptiness," which is the true nature of all phenomena. The realization of *prajna* also implies the attainment of enlightenment, and is in this sense one of the six *paramitas* or "perfections" of the *bodhisattva* path. Sometimes referred to by the compound term, *prajna-wisdom*.

Pure Land: Pure Land practice can be traced back to India and the teachings of the Buddha. It remains the most popular worldwide of all the 84,000 different Buddhist paths to supreme enlightenment. The Pure Land practitioner seeks rebirth in the Pure Land of Amitabha Buddha first through the cultivation of *bodhicitta*, or the aspiration for enlightenment; and second, through the practice of reciting the name of Amitabha Buddha with sincerity and deep devotion, and cultivating one's life through the three trainings of precepts, concentration, and *prajna*. Together, they enable one to more rapidly purify one's mind and liberate oneself from all delusions. Although one is not free from all wants and fears in the Pure Land, one is no longer bound by them. The Pure Land can also be found in this world with all its imperfections by the devout practitioner.

Samadhi: The highest state of mind achieved through meditation, chanting, reciting the Buddha's name, or other practices, in which the mind has reached ultimate concentration, so that it is no longer subject to thoughts and distractions. The highest state of *samadhi* is the "*bodhi*" or enlightened mind.

Sunyata: Literally "emptiness" or "void." This is a central concept in Buddhism, which asserts that everything existing in the world is due to dependent origination and has no permanent self or substance. Its meaning is twofold: 1) emptiness of living beings, which means that human beings or other living beings have no unchanging, substantial self; or 2) emptiness of *dharmas*, which means that the existence of all phenomena is due to causes and conditions. Unlike nihilism, this concept does not imply nothing exists, rather it stresses that all existence is without independent substance or absolute essence.

Sutra: Literally "threaded together." Refers to the scriptures taught directly by the Buddha and recorded by his disciples for all to follow in their practice. The direct assertion that these are the teachings of the Buddha is implied by the opening line of each sutra, "Thus have I heard."

Tathagata: Refers to one who has attained supreme enlightenment. The historical Sakyamuni Buddha used this title when speaking of himself or other Buddhas.

Ten Dharma Realms: These are the realms of: 1) hell, 2) hungry ghosts, 3) animals, 4) asuras, 5) humans, 6) heavens, 7) sravakas, 8) pratyekabuddhas, 9) bodhisattvas, and 10) Buddhas.

Ten Virtuous Practices: Buddhist teachings that instruct practitioners to: 1) protect and nurture life, 2) abstain from stealing, 3) abstain from sexual misconduct, 4) speak truthfully, 5) foster good relationships, 6) speak gently and use encouraging words, 7) speak sincerely, 8) practice generosity, 9) practice patience and tolerance, and 10) uphold the right view.

Theravada: Literally, "the teaching of the elders of the order" in Pali, referring to one of the eighteen schools during the Period of Sectarian Buddhism. Unlike the *bodhisattva* ideal in Mahayana tradition, this school's emphasis is on the liberation of the individual. In the 3rd century B.C.E., it was transmitted to Sri Lanka from India. Today it is popular in many areas of Southeast Asia.

About the Author
Venerable Master Hsing Yun

Founder of the Fo Guang Shan (Buddha's Light Mountain) Buddhist Order and the Buddha's Light International Association, Venerable Master Hsing Yun has dedicated his life to teaching Humanistic Buddhism, which seeks to realize spiritual cultivation in everyday living.

Master Hsing Yun is the 48th Patriarch of the Linji Chan School. Born in Jiangsu Province, China in 1927, he was tonsured under Venerable Master Zhikai at the age of twelve and became a novice monk at Qixia Vinaya College. He was fully ordained in 1941 following years of strict monastic training. When he left Jiaoshan Buddhist College at the age of twenty, he had studied for almost ten years in a monastery.

Due to the civil war in China, Master Hsing Yun moved to Taiwan in 1949 where he undertook the revitalization of Chinese Mahayana Buddhism. He began fulfilling his vow to promote the Dharma by starting chanting groups, student and youth groups, and other civic-minded organizations with Leiyin Temple in Ilan as his base. Since the founding of Fo Guang Shan monastery in Kaohsiung in 1967, more than two hundred temples have been established worldwide. Hsi Lai Temple, the symbolic torch of the Dharma spreading to the West, was built in 1988 near Los Angeles.'

Master Hsing Yun has been guiding Buddhism on a course of modernization by integrating Buddhist values into education, cultural activities, charity, and religious practices. To achieve these ends, he travels all over the world, giving lectures and actively engaging in religious dialogue. The Fo Guang Shan organization also oversees sixteen Buddhist colleges and four universities, one of which is the University of the West in Rosemead, California.

Over the past fifty years, Master Hsing Yun has written many books teaching Humanistic Buddhism and defining its practice. Whether providing insight into Buddhist sutras, human nature, or inter-religious exchange, he stresses the need for respect, compassion, and tolerance among all beings in order to alleviate suffering in this world. His works have been translated into English, French, German, Japanese, Korean, Portuguese, Russian, Spanish, Sinhalese, Thai, and Vietnamese.

About the Company

Buddha's Light Publishing
Fo Guang Shan International Translation Center

For as long as Venerable Master Hsing Yun has been a Buddhist monk, he has had a firm belief that books and other means of transmitting the Buddha's teachings can unite us spiritually, help us practice Buddhism at a higher altitude, and continuously challenge our views on how we define and live our lives.

In 1996, the Fo Guang Shan International Translation Center was established with this goal in mind. This marked the beginning of a series of publications translated into various languages from the Master's original writings in Chinese. Presently, several translation centers have been set up worldwide. Centers that coordinate translation or publication projects are located in Los Angeles, USA; Montreal, Canada; Sydney, Australia; Berlin, Germany; France; Sweden; Argentina; Brazil; South Africa; Japan; Korean; and Thailand.

In 2001, Buddha's Light Publishing was established to publish Buddhist books translated by Fo Guang Shan International Translation Center as well as other important Buddhist works. Buddha's Light Publishing is committed to building bridges between East and West, Buddhist communities, and cultures. All proceeds from our book sales support Buddhist propagation efforts.